CHORD PROGRESSIONS FOR THE TUNES

These chord progressions have been included to enable a teacher or other musician to improvise an accompaniment on the keyboard or guitar. They might also serve as source material for improvisation for flute players with a more advanced knowledge of harmony.

2 Blues for Beginners

$\frac{4}{4}$ | G7 | C7 | G7 | ∕. | C7 | ∕. | G7 | E7 | D7 | C7 | G7 | ∕. ‖

3 A la Mode

$\frac{4}{4}$ | Am7 Bm7 | C△7 Bm7 | Am7 Bm7 | C△7 Bm7 | Am7 Bm7 | C△7 Bm7 | Am7 | ∕. ‖

4 Progression

$\frac{4}{4}$ | F△7 | Em7 | Dm7 | C△7 | B♭△7 | Am7 | A♭△7 | ∕. :‖

5 Out for the Count

$\frac{4}{4}$ ▬ ‖: C7 | F7 | C7 | ∕. | F7 | F♯°7 | C/G* | A7 | Dm7 | G7 | 1. C7 A7 | Dm7 G7 :‖ 2. C7 | C7 ‖

6 Times Remembered

$\frac{4}{4}$ | C△7 | F♯m7♭5 B7 | C△7 | Gm7 C7 | F△7 | Fm7 B♭7 | Em7 E♭7 | 1. Dm7 D♭7 :‖ 2. C△7 | ∕. ‖

7 P.M.

$\frac{4}{4}$ | F△7 | Em7 | Dm7 | C△7 | F△7 | Em7 | Dm7 | C△7 :‖

8 Third Attempt

$\frac{4}{4}$ | F△7/G | Em7/G | F△7/G | Em7/G | F△7/G | Em7/G | F△7/F | Em7/G :‖

9 Flat 5

$\frac{4}{4}$ | G13 | ∕. | F13 | ∕. | G13 | ∕. | F13 | ∕. | ∕. ‖

10 Interstellar

$\frac{4}{4}$ | F♯m7♭5 | B7 | Dm7 | G7 | Gm7 | C7 | F△7 | ∕. ‖

*An oblique sign / means that the following note is to be played as the bass of the chord.

11 251

4/4 Dm7 | G7 | CΔ7 | C#° | Dm7 | G7 | CΔ7 | A7 :‖ **1.** **2.** CΔ7 ‖

12 Home Bass

4/4 – ‖: G G/B | C7 C#° | G/D Em7 | Am7 D7 | G G/B | C7 C#° | G/D Em7 | Am7 D7 :‖ G | ∕ ‖

13 James

4/4 DΔ7 | CΔ7 | DΔ7 | CΔ7 | FΔ7 | Em7 | Dm7 | C#Δ7 | ∕ ‖

14 South View

4/4 6x G | C | D | G :‖

15 Minor Problem

4/4 G#m7♭5 C#7♭9 | F#m7 | Bm7 E7 | AΔ7 | G#m7♭5 C#7♭9 | F#m7 A7 | D7 C#7♭9 | F#m7 (D#m7♭5) :‖

16 Roberto

4/4 Em7♭5 | E♭7 | Dm7 | C#° | Cm7 | F7 | B♭Δ7 | ∕ :‖

17 Delta City

4/4 – ‖: G7 | ∕ | ∕ | ∕ | C7 | ∕ | G7 | ∕ | D7 | ∕ | C7 | ∕ | G7 | ∕ | ∕ | ∕ :‖ **1.** **2.** G7 | ∕ ‖

18 Gangsterland

4/4 ⟨4⟩ ⫟ ‖: B♭7 B7 | C7 | F7 F#7 | G7 :‖ B♭13 | A13 | F7 F#7 | G7 |

C13 B13 | B♭13 | **1.** A7 E♭7 | D7 – ‖: **2.** F7 F#7 | G7 :‖ F7 F#7 | G7 𝄾 – ‖
D.S.

19 Breaking Point

4/4 B♭13 | Am7 | B♭13 | Am7 | B♭13 | Am7 Gm7 | FΔ7 | ∕ ‖

20 Transition

4/4 Dm7 | C/E | FΔ7 | C/E | Dm7 | C/E | FΔ7 | F#Δ7#11 | ∕ ‖

21 Sylvie's Dance

4/4 AΔ7 | GΔ7 | AΔ7 | GΔ7 | AΔ7 | GΔ7 | CΔ7 C6 | CΔ7 C6 :‖

22 K.O.

$\frac{4}{4}$ ⅊ | Dm7 | Em7♭5 A7 | Dm7 | ✗ | Gm7 | C7 | F△7 | Bb△7 |

Em7♭5 | A7 | Dm7 | F7 | Em7♭5 | A7 | Dm7 | ✗ ‖

23 Blue Jean

$\frac{4}{4}$ — ‖: Am7 | Bm7♭5 E7♭9 | Am7 | Em7♭5 A7 | Dm7 | G7 | C△7 |

F△7 | Bm7♭5 | E7♭9 | **1.** Am7 C7 | Bm7♭5 E7♭9 :‖ **2.** Am7 | ✗ ‖

24 Improvisation in F

$\frac{4}{4}$ Bb△7 | Am7 | Gm7 | F△7 :‖

25 Devil Music

$\frac{4}{4}$ ⅊ | Eb9♭5 | Ab9 | Eb9♭5 | Bbm7 Eb7 | Ab9♭5 | A° | Eb7♭5 | C7 | F7 | B7 | Bb7 | E7 | Eb7 | — Eb13 ‖

26 Bird Waltz (C major)

$\frac{3}{4}$ C△7 | Bm7♭5 E7 | Am7 D7 | Gm7 C7 | F△7 | Fm7 | Em7 | Ebm7 | Dm7 | G7 | **1.** Db△7 | ✗ :‖ **2.** C△7 | ✗ ‖

27 Bird Waltz (B major)

$\frac{3}{4}$ B△7 | Bbm7♭5 Eb7 | Abm7 Db7 | F#m7 B7 | E△7 | Em7 | Ebm7 | Dm7 | C#m7 | F#7 | **1.** C△7 | ✗ :‖ **2.** B△7 | ✗ ‖

28 A Song for Sophie

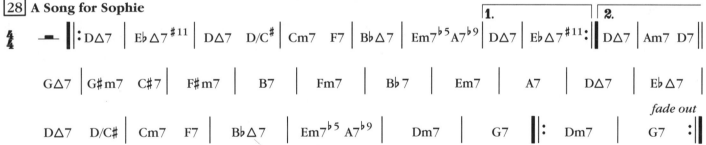

$\frac{4}{4}$ — ‖: D△7 | Eb△7#11 | D△7 D/C# | Cm7 F7 | Bb△7 | Em7♭5 A7♭9 | **1.** D△7 | Eb△7#11 :‖ **2.** D△7 | Am7 D7 ‖

G△7 | G#m7 C#7 | F#m7 | B7 | Fm7 | Bb7 | Em7 | A7 | D△7 | Eb△7 |

D△7 D/C# | Cm7 F7 | Bb△7 | Em7♭5 A7♭9 | Dm7 | G7 ‖: Dm7 | G7 :‖

fade out

29 The House in the Forest

$\frac{4}{4}$ C△7 | G7sus4 | C△7 | G7 sus4 ‖: C△7 | G7 sus4 | C△7 | Fm7 Bb7 | Eb△7 | Dm7 G7#5 |

1. C△7 | G7 sus4 :‖ **2.** C△7 | Bm7 E7 | Am7 | Bm7 E7 | Am7 | F#m7♭5 B7 | Em7 | F#m7 B7 |

Em7 A7 | Dm7 | G7 ‖ C△7 | G7 sus4 | Em7♭5 | A7 | Dm7 | C#△7 | C△7 | G7 sus4 ‖: C△7 | G7 sus4 :‖

fade out

30 Tongue-Twister

$\frac{4}{4}$ A7 | ∤ | ∤ | ∤ | D7 | ∤ | A7 | ∤ | E7 | D7 | A7 | ∤ ‖

31 Lullaby

$\frac{4}{4}$ F△7 | F△7^{b5} | Em7 | Am7/E | Dm7 | G7^{sus4} | C△7 | C7 | F△7 | F△7^{b5} | Em7 | Am7 | Dm7 | Db△7 | C△7 | ∤ ‖
Fine

Bb13$^{\#11}$ | ∤ | C△7 | ∤ | Bb13$^{\#11}$ | ∤ | C△7 | ∤ | Bb13$^{\#11}$ | ∤ | C△7 | Eb13 | Dm7 | Db7 | C△7 | C7 ‖
D.C. al Fine

32 Moon Tune

$\frac{4}{4}$ G△7 | Gm7 C7 | F△7 | Fm7 Bb7 | Eb△7 | D7^{sus4} | Eb△7 | Am7 D7 :‖ | **1.** Eb△7 | Am7 D7 :‖ | **2.** Eb△7 | Ab△7$^{\#11}$ | G△7 ‖

33 The Loneliest Monk

$\frac{4}{4}$ Eb7 | Ab7 | Eb7 | Bbm7 | Eb7 | Ab7 | A° | Eb7 | Db7 | C7 | Fm7 | Bb7 | Eb7 Gb7 | F7 E7 | Eb9 ‖

34 Improvisation in G

$\frac{3}{4}$ G△7/D | Am7/D | Bm7/D | Am7/D :‖

35 The Magician

$\frac{4}{4}$ ⁊ − ‖: Am Am/G | F7 E7 | Am Am/G | F7 E7 | Am Am/G | F7 E7 | Am C7 | Bm7^{b5} E7^{b9} :‖

2. Am | ∤ ‖ Dm7 | G13 | Am7 | F#m7^{b5} | Bm7^{b5} | F13 | E7 | Bb13 ‖
D.S. al Coda

CODA
Am | F7 | E7 | Am | F7 | E7 | Am ‖

36 'Trane Refrain

$\frac{4}{4}$ ⁊ ‖: Em7 F#m7 | G△7 F#m7 | Em7 F#m7 | G△7 F#m7 | Am7 Bm7 | C△7 Bm7 | Em7 F#m7 |

G△7 F#m7 | C13 | B13 | **1.** Em7 F#m7 | G△7 F#m7 :‖ **2.** Em7 | ∤ ‖

37 Blue Monk

3x
$\frac{4}{4}$ Bb7 | Eb7 | Bb7 | ∤ | Eb7 | ∤ | Bb7 | G7 | Cm7 | F7 | Bb7 | ∤ :‖

4

38 | A Bossa for Betty

𝄢 4/4 | Dm6 | Em7♭5 A7 | Dm6 | Em7♭5 A7 | Dm6 | Em7♭5 A7 | Dm6 | ℅ | Gm7 | C7 |

| F△7 | B♭△7 | Em7♭5 | A7 | Dm7 | G7 | Cm7 | F7 | E13 | A7♭9 ‖

D.S. al Coda

CODA

Dm7 | F7 ‖: Em7♭5 | A7♭9 | Dm7 | F7 :‖ Em7♭5 | A7♭9 | Dm6 | ℅ ‖

39 | Sister Caroline

4/4 ‖: E♭7 | A♭7 | E♭7 | ℅ | A♭7 | A°7 | E♭7 | ℅ | B♭13 | A♭13 | E♭7 | ℅ :‖

40 | Happy Feet

4/4 | D13 | ℅ | C13 | ℅ | D13 | ℅ | C13 | ℅ ‖: D13 | ℅ | C13 | ℅ |

1.
D13 | ℅ | G13 | ℅ :‖ **2.** D13 | A♭13 | G13 | G13 A13 | D13 | ℅ ‖

C13 | ℅ | D13 | ℅ | C13 B13 | B♭13 | A13 | ℅ ‖: D13 | ℅ | C13 | ℅ :‖ *fade out*

41 | Aikido

4/4 ‖: Cm7 | F7 | Cm7 | F7 | Fm7 | B♭7 | Cm7 | F7 | Dm7 | G7 | Cm7 |

F7 | E♭m7 | A♭7 | Dm7 | G7 :‖ Cm7 | F7 | Cm7 | F7 | Cm7 ‖

42 | Red Alert

4/4 | F13 | ℅ | E♭13 | ℅ | D♭13 | ℅ | C13 | ℅ :‖: F7 | B♭7 | F7 | Cm7 F7 | B♭7 | ℅ |

F7 | D7 | Gm7 | C7 | F7 A♭7 | G7 G♭7 :‖

D.S. al Coda

CODA
C7 | F7 ‖

43 | I Will Call You

3/4 | G△7 | C△7 | F△7 | Em7 | F△7 | B♭△7 | E♭△7#11 | D7sus4 ‖ G△7 | C△7 | Bm7 | Bm/A | G#m7♭5 |

C#7♭9 | F#△7 | ℅ ‖ G#m7 | C#7 | F#△7 | F#△6 | F#m7 | B7 | E△7 | E△6 ‖ Em7 | A7 | D△7 |

G△7 | C△7 | Bm7 | Am7 | D7 ‖ **CODA** B♭△7 | E♭△7 | A♭△7 | Gm7 | A♭△7 | Gm7 A♭△7 ‖: Gm7 | A♭△7 :‖ *fade out*

D.C. al Coda

5

44 The Bottom Line

$\frac{4}{4}$ | Bb13 | ⁄. | Am7 | ⁄. | AbΔ7 | ⁄. | Gsus4 | ⁄. :‖

45 Oh When the Saints Go Marching In

$\frac{4}{4}$ ⁅ — | DbΔ7 | B13 | Bbm7 Bbm7/Ab | Gm7b5 F#Δ7 | Fm7 | Bb7#9 E7b13 | Eb13 Eb7 b13 #11 b9 ‖

| Ab9 | Abm7 | Db7 | F#Δ7 | B13 | Fm7 Bb7 | Ebm7 Absus4 | DΔ7 | ⌢ DbΔ7 ‖

46 Claret and Blue

$\frac{4}{4}$ | A7 | D7 | A7 | ⁄. | D7 | G7 | A7 | ⁄. | E7 | D7 | A7 | ⁄. ‖

47 Country Road

$\frac{3}{4}$ | F7 | B7 | Bb7 | C7 :‖ Bb7 | B° | F7 | Ab7 | G7 | Db7 | C7 | Gb7 ‖

| F7 | B7 | Bb7 | C7 | F7 | Ab13 | G7 | GbΔ7 | B13#11 | ⁄. ‖

48 Euphrates

$\frac{3}{4}$ Dm7 ⁄ ⁄. (4) ⁄ ⁄ ⁄. (8) ‖: Dm7 ⁄ ⁄. (4) ⁄ ⁄ ⁄. (8) ‖ Ebm7 ⁄ ⁄. (4) ⁄ ⁄ ⁄. (8) |

| Gm6 | C7 | ⁄ (4) | ⁄ | ⁄ | Dm7 | ⁄. | ⁄. (4) | ⁄. | ⁄. | ⁄. | ⁄. (8) *fade out* :‖: Dm7 ⁄. |

49 Endless Night

$\frac{4}{4}$ ⁅ ‖: Cm | ⁄. | Bb6 | ⁄. | AbΔ7 | ⁄. | G7 | ⁄. :‖ |1. ... |2. AbΔ7 | G7#5 b9 | Cm | ⁄. ‖

| Ab7 | G7#9 b13 | Cm | Eb7 | Dm7b5 | AbΔ7 | G7sus4 | G7 ‖ **CODA** AbΔ7 | G7#5 b9 | Cm | ⁄. ‖

D.S. al Coda

50 My Little Suede Shoes

$\frac{4}{4}$ — 8 — ‖: Fm7 Bb7 | EbΔ7 | Fm7 Bb7 | EbΔ7 | Fm7 Bb7 | Gm7 C7 | Fm7 Bb7 | EbΔ7 :‖

| AbΔ7 | Gm7 | Fm7 Bb7 | EbΔ7 | AbΔ7 | Gm7 | Fm7 Bb7 | EbΔ7 ‖

D.S. al Coda

CODA
| Gm7 C7 | Fm7 Bb7 | EbΔ7 | Fm7 Bb7 | EbΔ7 | Fm7 Bb7 EbΔ7 ‖

51 Doxy

$\frac{4}{4}$ ⁊ | Bb7 | Ab7 G7 | C7 | F7 | Bb | Bb7 | Ab7 G7 | C7 | F7 |

| Bb7 | ⁄. | Eb7 | E° | Bb7 | Ab7 G7 | C7 | F7 | Bb ‖

52 I'm In Love

$\frac{4}{4}$ Ab/Bb | ℀. | ℀. | Bb+7♭9 ‖ EbΔ | Gm7 C7 | Fm7 D7/F# | Eb/G G7 |

AbΔ G7 | G7 Cm7 | F7 | Fm7 Bb7 ‖ EbΔ | Dm7♭5 G7 | Cm B7 | Bbm7 A7 |

AbΔ | Gm7♭5 C7♭9 | Fm7 C7 | B7♭5 Bb7♭9 ‖ EbΔ | Gm7 C7 | Fm7 D7/F# |

Eb/G G7 | AbΔ G7 | G7 Cm7 | F7 | Bbm7 Eb7 Eb7+ ‖ AbΔ | Gm7 C7+ |

C7♭9 Fm7 | F#m7 B7 | Gm7 C7 | B7 Bb7 | DbΔ D° | Eb | ‖: Ab/Bb :‖
fade out

53 Tango Cool

$\frac{4}{4}$ Gm7 | EbΔ7 :‖‖: Gm7 | EbΔ7 | Gm7 | EbΔ7 | Gm7 | EbΔ7 | AbΔ7 | D7♭9 :‖

EbΔ7 D7♭9 | Gm7 | EbΔ7 | Gm7 | EbΔ7 ‖ AbΔ7 | Am7♭5 D7♭9 | Gm7 |

Fm7 Bb7 | Eb7#9 | D7♭9 | Gm7 | EbΔ7 | Gm7 | EbΔ7 | Gm | ℀. ‖

54 Frankincense

$\frac{4}{4}$ Gm7 | C7 | Am7 | Ab7♭5 | Gm7 | C7 | Am7 | Bm7 E7 | Bbm7 | Eb7 | Cm7♭5 | F7 |

Fine

Gm7 | C7 | F (F+) | F6 ‖ F#m7 | B7♭5 | Am7 | D7 | Cm7 | F7 | Bm7 E7 | Bbm7 Eb7 ‖
D.C. al Fine

55 Peace

$\frac{4}{4}$ ⁊ ‖: Am7♭5 D7♭9 | Gm7 C7 | BΔ7 Cm7♭5 F7#9 | BbΔ7 | Bm7 E7 |

AΔ7 A/G# F#m7 F#m/E | Ebm7♭5 D7♭5 | DbΔ7 | C7♭5 B7♭5 | BbΔ7 :‖

56 Triad Exercise

fade out

$\frac{4}{4}$ C | F | G7 | C :‖

57 Mingus-Thingus

$\frac{6}{8}$ ⁊ ⁊ ⁊ ‖: A7 | ℀ | ℀ | ℀ | D7 | ℀ | A7 | ℀ | F13 |

[1.] E13 | A7 | ℀ | F13 | E13 | A7 | ℀ :‖ [2.] F13 | E13 | A7 | A7 ‖

58 Pan Pipes

§

$\frac{5}{4}$ Fm7 Bb7 | ℀ | ℀ | ℀ ‖: ℀ | ℀ | ℀ | ℀ | ℀ | ℀ | ℀ :‖
⊕

CODA *fade out*

Bbm7 | Eb7 | AbΔ7 | DbΔ7 | Bbm7 Eb7 | Gm7♭5 | C7 ‖ ‖: Fm7 | Bb7 ‖

D.S. al coda without repeat

7

59 Straight, No Chaser

4/4 𝄆 Bb7 | Eb7 | Bb7 | ∕. | Eb7 | ∕. | Bb7 | ∕. | Cm7 | F7 | Bb7 | ∕. 𝄇

60 Fall '90

4/4 𝄆 Dm7 | G7 | CΔ7 | FΔ7 | Bm7♭5 | E7 | Am6 | ∕. 𝄇 Bm7♭5 | E7 |
Am6 | ∕. | Dm7 | G7 | CΔ7 | FΔ7 | Bm7♭5 | E7 | Am7 D7 | Gm7 C7 |
𝄆 F7 | E7 | Am6 | F#m7♭5 𝄇 F7 | E7 | Am6 | ∕. 𝄇

61 Danny Boy

4/4 CΔ7 Gm7 C7 | FΔ7 Dm Bb¹³/9 | Em7 A7 | D13 D7♭¹³ G9 G7♭9 |
CΔ7 Gm7 C7 | FΔ7 Dm Bb¹³/9 | Em7 Am7 Dm7 G7sus4 | CΔ7 G11 G/F |
C/E FΔ7 | CΔ7/G G#° Am G11 G/F | C/E FΔ7 | Ab7♭5 Gsus4 |
Gm7/C C7 FΔ7 F#° | C/G G#° Am F7 | Em7 Am7 Dm7 G7 | Db Δ7 CΔ7 𝄇

62 St Thomas

2/2 [8] 𝄆 C | Em7♭5 A7♭9 | Dm7 G7 | C G7 | C | Em7♭5 A7♭9 | Dm7 G7 |
C G7 | C Bb7 | A7 | Dm7 Dm/C | G/B G7 | C C/E | F7 F#° | G7 | C 𝄇

63 Blue Samba

¢ [20] F#7 | B7 | F#7 | ∕. | B7 | ∕. | F#7 | ∕. |
𝄆 C#7 | B7 | F#7 | ∕. 𝄇 C#7 | B7 | F#7 ‖

64 It's All Yours

4/4 Gm Gm/F# | Gm/F C7 | FΔ7 Bb7 | Am7 Ab° | Gm7 Gm/F | Em7♭5 A7 | Dm7 Gm7 C7 |
[1.] FΔ7 Am7♭5 D7 𝄇 [2.] FΔ7 Abm7 Db7 ‖ Gb Δ7 Abm7 | Bbm7 Bm7 E7 | Bbm7 Eb Abm7 Db |
Gb Δ7 | F#m7 B7 | EΔ7 G° | F#m7 B7 | E7 Eb7 D7 Ab7 | Gm Gm/F# | Gm/F C7 |
FΔ7 Bb7 | Am7 Ab° | Gm7 Gm/F | Em7♭5 A7 | Dm7 Gm7 C7 | FΔ7 ‖

65 On the Street

4/4 C7 | Gm7 | C7 | Gm7 | Cm7 F7 | Bb7 Eb7 | Am7♭5 D7♭9 | Gm7 𝄇 Cm7 B7 |
Bb Δ7 G7#5 | Cm7 F7 | Bb Δ7 Bb6 | G7 Ab7 G7 Cm6 | Em7♭5 A7 Em7♭5 A7 | Ebm7 Ab7 Dm7♭5 G7 ‖

fade out

C7 | Gm7 | C7 | Gm7 | Cm7 F7 | Bb7 Eb7 | Am7♭5 D7♭9 | Gm7 𝄆 C7 | Gm7 𝄇

John O'Neill

*Dedicated to Richard Rowland,
in memory of good times spent
listening to music together.*

SCHOTT
EDUCATIONAL
PUBLICATIONS

ACKNOWLEDGEMENTS

Many of the ideas in this book were inspired by four great teachers: Don Rendell, who took me under his wing when I was just beginning; Peter Ind, who introduced me to the concepts of Lennie Tristano and told me to listen to Pat Metheny; Lee Konitz, who gave me a new direction and discipline for my improvisation; and the late Warne Marsh.

I would also like to thank the following people:

Phil Lee, Jeff Clyne, Paul Clarvis and Andy Panayi for their superb musicianship, professionalism, patience and creative contribution during the recording of the CD.

The staff at Schott & Co. Ltd.

All the musicians who gave permission for their compositions to be included in this book.

All my students, who played such an important part in shaping the book.

Nick Taylor of Porcupine Studio for his engineering and mixing.

Henry Binns for his photographs.

John Minnion for his line drawings.

Bob Glass of Ray's Jazz Shop for his help in compiling the discography.

Willie Garnett for looking after my instruments.

My family and friends for their unwavering support and belief.

British Library Cataloguing-in-Publication Data. A catalogue record for this book is available from the British Library

ISBN 0 946535 24 8

© 1994 Schott & Co. Ltd, London

Designed and typeset by Geoffrey Wadsley
Cover: Herbie Mann (photograph by David Redfern) © Redferns, London

CONTENTS

The publishers would like to thank the following for allowing the use of their material in this publication:
John Minnion for the illustrations.
Henry Binns for the technical photographs.
Ted Gioia, Lee Konitz, Andrew Panayi and Don Rendell for their compositions.
Bocu Music Ltd, BMG Music Publishing Ltd, Marada Music Ltd and Prestige Music Ltd for their copyright music.
The author and publishers also wish to acknowledge, with thanks, Redferns Music Picture Library/Photographers: David Redfern (Roland Kirk, p. 15; Lew Tabackin, p. 15; Bud Shank, p. 15; James Moody, p. 15; Frank Foster with the Count Basie Band, p. 21; Stan Getz, p. 27; Miles Davis, p. 39; John Coltrane, p. 50; Horace Silver, p. 73; Dave Brubeck Quartet, p. 74; Charles Lloyd, p. 92), William Gottlieb (Louis Armstrong, p. 42; Thelonious Monk, p. 47; Charlie Parker, p. 67), Charles Stewart (Eric Dolphy, p. 93).
© Redferns, London

HOW TO USE THIS BOOK

Mastery of the foundation techniques presented in Part One is the key to playing the flute well, so please ensure you are comfortable with the exercises in this section of the book before attempting the pieces in Part Two.

Many of the chapters finish with suggestions for further listening, reading or practice. You are advised to adopt as many of these suggestions as possible in order to gain maximum benefit from the method.

If your speakers are connected properly the rhythm section will be heard from the left speaker and the flute from the right speaker. By using the 'balance' controls on your music system you will therefore be able to adjust the 'mix' between flute and rhythm section, or indeed to filter out the flute completely. This means you can choose to play with or without the flute for guidance. There are also several pieces which give you the further option of playing a duet part.

You should not expect to be able to play every piece immediately with the CD. It may require several hours of practice to work some of the music up to speed. If the music is too fast do not struggle to play with the recorded accompaniment—such practice is fruitless and frustrating. It is far better to practise **slowly**—at half-speed or even slower—and gradually build up to the challenge of playing with the CD.

It is particularly important that you develop your ear as well as your technique and ability to read. With this in mind try to play by ear as much as possible, for example by memorizing the tunes after you have learnt to read them or by transposing them into other keys or different registers of the instrument.

This book is not a rigid 'classical' method. Once you have learnt to play what is written you should feel free to alter rhythms, embellish or improvise. Many of the tunes will benefit from being treated in this way.

Above all ENJOY YOURSELF!

SOME THOUGHTS ABOUT PRACTICE

Try to make the environment you practise in as pleasant as possible. The room should be bright and well ventilated. It should also preferably not be too cluttered—if there is a lack of bare wall space the room will lack resonance and your sound will be deadened. Soft furnishings like thick carpets and curtains have a particularly muffling effect. On the other hand this might be an advantage if your neighbours complain about the noise!

It is very important to practise regularly—every day if possible. 20 minutes a day is much more valuable than one or two much longer sessions a week.

If you practise more intensively remember that it is more effective to play for short periods of 20 minutes to half an hour with breaks in between than to play for hours at a stretch.

Do not expect to progress at a uniform rate, however hard you practise. The foundation techniques in particular can take a long time to master. Very often you will encounter the 'plateau effect', where you feel for a long time that you are not progressing at all. Do not be discouraged! Such periods are nearly always followed by a dramatic leap forward.

Avoid practising when you are tired. It may be more effective to practise at the beginning or middle of the day than at the end if your lifestyle permits.

Do not practise in a half-hearted way—you will be wasting your time.

Warm up properly—long notes or simple tonguing exercises are ideal.

You can do a lot of valuable practice without the instrument in your hands—singing, clapping or listening to music for example.

Avoid becoming obsessed by any one aspect of your playing—there are many different skills to acquire.

Fear of failure is the biggest enemy, and usually what gets in the way of people achieving their musical potential. You must learn to trust that all problems can be overcome by practising with the right attitude. Believe in yourself.

ABOUT THE FLUTE

The word 'flute' is a very general word which, according to *The New Grove Dictionary*, is used to refer to 'any instrument having an air column confined in a hollow body and activated by a stream of air from the player's lips striking against the sharp edge of an opening'. Different kinds of flutes were played in many ancient civilizations and continue to be played in different cultures throughout the modern world.

There is evidence to suggest that the oldest *transverse* or cross-blown, flute was the chinese *ch'ih*, which can be traced to the ninth century BC. The flute first appeared in Western Europe in Germanic lands and was established as a solo voice during the Baroque period, most notably through the works of J. S. Bach, Handel, Telemann and Vivaldi. The instrument which they wrote for was wooden, with only one key, but underwent various technical modifications until, in the middle of the nineteenth century, it was completely redesigned by Theobald Boehm, and transformed into an instrument which closely resembles the modern orchestral flute. Very little was composed for the instrument by any of the great nineteenth-century composers, but in the twentieth century there has been a resurgence of interest and the list of those who have written for it includes such eminent figures as Debussy, Hindemith, Milhaud, Prokofiev, Poulenc, Vaughan Williams, Neilsen, Berio, Boulez and Rodrigo.

With the exception of saxophonist Wayman Carver, who played flute as his second instrument, making recordings with the bands of Benny Carter and Chick Webb in the 1930s, and who therefore might be regarded as the first jazz flutist, very little jazz was played on the flute before the 1950s. Its low volume and lack of penetration by comparison with instruments such as the trumpet and saxophone made it difficult for it to find a role in the exuberant idioms of New Orleans, Swing and Bebop. However, with the advent in the 1950s of the generally softer sound of the West Coast or 'Cool' style, the flute began to interest composers, arrangers and players. At the same time jazz began to be strongly influenced by Latin American music, in which the flute had always played a significant part. This decade also saw the emergence of Herbie Mann, the first jazz player to make a successful career for himself with flute as his primary instrument.

In subsequent years an increasing number of musicians have specialized on the flute, and while the instrument has never been as prominent as the saxophone or trumpet as a solo voice, it has gained in popularity to the extent that most saxophonists make the flute their second instrument in preference to the clarinet. With the increasing influence of World Music it would seem likely that the flute, which has strong associations with different kinds of ethnic music, is to remain an important tone colour in jazz.

FURTHER STUDY

Reading:

JOACHIM E. BERENDT, *The Jazz Book*
BARRY KERNFELD, ed., *The New Grove Dictionary of Jazz*
STANLEY SADIE, ed., *The New Grove Dictionary of Music and Musicians*

Part One:
The Foundation Techniques

BREATHING EXERCISES

Good breathing technique is essential for flute playing. The following exercises will help to develop this.

Stand in front of a mirror, preferably one in which you can see yourself from the waist up. Breathe in through the mouth. You may have raised the shoulders and lifted the chest to accomplish this. For the purposes of woodwind playing this is both unnecessary and incorrect. Nor is it how you breathe when you allow unconscious processes to take over.

Exercise 1
Take hold of an average sized hardback book, lie on the floor on your back, place the book on your abdomen and relax (Fig. 1). Do not try to breathe in any special way. Simply observe the natural breathing process. You will notice that the book rises as you breathe in and falls as you breathe out. In other words **expansion on inhaling, contraction on exhaling.**

Fig. 1

Now all you have to do is achieve this in a vertical rather than a horizontal position and as a slightly more controlled, conscious process.

Fig. 2

Exercise 2
- Place the hands on the abdomen (Fig. 2).
- Breathe in through the mouth—a small sip of air rather than a massive gulp. The hands should be pushed out slightly. Exhale.
- Now place the hands on the back (Fig. 3). Breathe in again. You should notice that the hands are pushed backwards. It is as if you were breathing in through two holes in the back underneath the hands. The point is that you are not simply pushing the stomach out but achieving all-round expansion in the area of the waist and lower ribs.

Fig. 3

This kind of breathing is called diaphragm breathing. The diaphragm is the powerful muscular floor to the chest cavity. In correct deep breathing the diaphragm moves down to make room as the lungs inflate, thus bringing about the expansion described.

You must now turn your attention to the exhalation. The diaphragm is like a piece of elastic. Left to its own devices it will simply spring back into position and the exhalation will be very short-lived. You might liken this effect to blowing up a balloon and then letting go of it. The balloon flies around the room and within seconds has emptied itself of air. If you let go of your breath in an uncontrolled way your note on the flute will be as erratic and short-lived as the flight of the balloon! You must exert a braking influence on the upward movement of the diaphragm, and do this by contracting the muscles which surround it.

Here is an exercise for practising control of these muscles:

Exercise 3
- Breathe in (as described in Exercise 2 above).
- Now breathe out making a loud whispered 'ah' sound. Keep the throat open and relaxed. The 'ah' should be as long and steady as possible—ten or fifteen seconds would be reasonable for a beginner.

What you should notice is that the muscles around the diaphragm squeeze more and more firmly until the breath runs out. This effect can be likened to squeezing out a sponge. If you wish to achieve a steady flow of water you must squeeze first gently and then ever more tightly.

In flute playing the sound is created by the air-jet being split into two equal parts by the far edge of the embouchure hole (see Fig. 4). The sound thus produced is called an **edge-tone**. Exactly the same principle is at work when sound is produced by blowing across the top of a bottle. You should always bear in mind that you are trying to create an edge-tone.

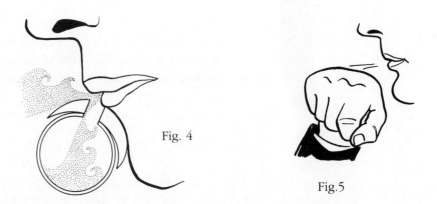

Fig. 4

Fig.5

It is not only the **direction** of the air-jet but also its **velocity** which is critical. An edge-tone will only be produced if the air-jet is moving quickly enough. The following exercises, which you can practise whenever you have a spare moment, will demonstrate how you can influence both the velocity and direction of the air which you blow:

Hold your hand just below your mouth (see Fig. 5), compress the lips as if you were about to say the letter 'p' and blow air onto the back of the hand through a small hole at the centre of your lips. The air-jet should feel cold—a sign that the air is moving with sufficient velocity. If it feels warm you are blowing either too gently or through too large a hole. **When playing the flute you should always think of blowing cold air.**

Now try to move this cold jet of air backwards and forwards across your hand. To achieve this you will need to alter the position of the lower lip in relation to the upper one. When the lower lip is further back the air-jet will be directed more downwards; as the lip moves forward the air is directed further away from you. When playing the flute you will constantly be making subtle changes to the angle of the air-jet.

BLOWING ON THE HEAD JOINT

As a beginner flute player you will probably be keen to put the instrument together and start trying to play some tunes. However, since the most difficult challenge is to produce a good sound, it would be far better for you to spend at least one week blowing on **just the head joint**, without having to worry about other factors like posture or fingering.

● Take hold of the head joint of the flute and position yourself in front of a mirror so that you get a good **close-up** view of your mouth. If you can arrange it so that you can also get a side-view by using a second mirror that would be even better.

● Press the lip plate **firmly** but comfortably into the indentation between the lower lip and the chin and rotate the head joint until the edge of the lip, where the red part meets the white, is just inside the inner edge of the embouchure hole (see Fig. 4).

- Inhale, in the same way as you have learnt from the breathing exercises, and press the lips together, imagining you are about to say the letter 'p'. The corners of the mouth should feel firm but relaxed, neither pulling back nor pushing in.
- Try to exhale, but for the moment **keeping the lips together**, so that you experience the breath pressure building up behind the lips. The muscles around the diaphragm should be contracted, supporting the breath.
- Allow the breath pressure to force the lips **slightly** apart, so that a small aperture is formed at the centre of the lips, and direct the air-jet at the far edge of the embouchure hole (see Fig. 4). You may find it helpful to imagine the syllable 'pe' as in the word 'perhaps' when attempting this.

Experiment with rotating the head joint inwards and outwards, listening for the purest and strongest sound. In theory you should cover approximately one third of the embouchure hole with your lower lip, when blowing on the head joint alone.

You should also experiment with varying the distance between the lips and the embouchure hole.

- Once you have established a good note sustain it for as long as possible, trying to produce a completely even tone, which does not vary in pitch or volume. This can only be achieved by a correct breathing technique, as outlined in Exercise 3 of the breathing exercises.

ASSEMBLING & DISASSEMBLING THE INSTRUMENT

Take hold of the head joint in one hand and the top part of the body tube in the other and ease the head joint into the body tube making sure that you **do not exert pressure on the key rods** (see Fig. 6). If the joints are stiff clean with a tissue both parts of the metal which come into contact. Rotate the head joint until the embouchure hole is aligned with the majority of keys on the body tube (see Fig. 7).

Holding the foot joint at the bottom to avoid exerting pressure on the rods, attach it to the body tube (see Fig. 8), so that the main rod of the foot joint is in line with the centre of the lowest key on the body tube (see Fig. 7). The flute is now assembled.

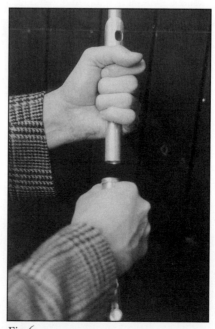

Fig.6

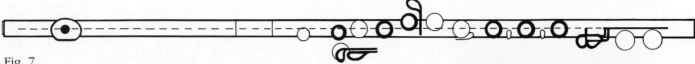

Fig. 7

Disassembly is a straightforward reversal of the above procedure. If moisture is allowed to remain inside the instrument it may shorten the life of the pads, and should therefore be removed by inserting a small piece of soft cloth or chamois leather in the 'eye' of the cleaning rod—which is usually provided with the instrument—and pulling it through the different sections of the flute.

Fig.8

HAND POSITION AND POSTURE

The flute is **balanced**, **not held**, by means of a lever system. The left hand index finger serves as the fulcrum, while the right hand thumb and little finger, in conjunction with the whole of the right arm, push outwards (see Fig. 9), so that the lip plate is held firmly in position underneath the lower lip. In order to achieve this observe the following points:

Fig. 9

- The index finger of the left hand should be crooked and pulled as far back as it will comfortably go (see Fig. 10).
- The flute should be positioned against the base of the index finger, just above the knuckle joint (see Fig. 10).
- Because the right thumb is **pushing rather than lifting** it should be positioned not directly underneath the flute but slightly further back (see Fig. 11).
- The little finger of the right hand depresses the E♭ key and pushes outwards in the same way as the right thumb (see Fig. 12). Make sure you do not overlook this when interpreting the fingering diagrams.
- Both elbows should be well away from the body (see Figs. 13 and 14). This will allow the chest to open, thus promoting correct breathing technique, and is also

Fig.11

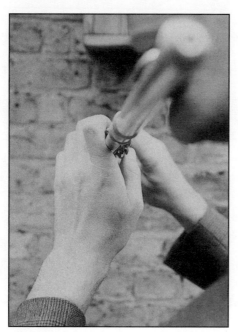

Fig.10

Fig.12

necessary in order to sustain the forward push of the right arm. On no account should you resort to trying to provide extra support by holding the left elbow against the side of the body.

Good posture is of vital importance. Stand with the feet approximately the same distance apart as your shoulders and the weight distributed evenly on the soles of both feet. Turn the hips and upper body to the left—this should feel natural since the right arm is already pushing outwards (see Figs. 10, 13 and 14).

Fig. 13

Fig. 14

The chin should be drawn in and the head tilted slightly forwards in order to induce a feeling of length in the back of the neck. Imagine you are a puppet being drawn up towards the ceiling by a string attached to the crown of your head—this should help your posture to feel light and relaxed.

● The fleshy pad at the end of the finger should make contact with the key (see Fig. 15).
● The fingers should be gently curved, not flat or contracted (see Fig. 15).

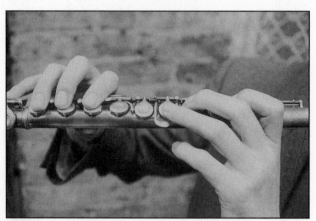

Fig.15

● The fingers move by means of a hammer action which is initiated at the knuckle joint. Movement of the other finger joints should be kept to a minimum.
● The fingers should stay as close as possible to the keys. Do not waste energy!
● In order for the fingers to stay relaxed and move efficiently the neck muscles, shoulder joints, elbows and wrists should also be relaxed.

TONE DEVELOPMENT

You should now practise long notes in front of a mirror with the flute fully assembled, following the same procedure that you adopted for blowing on the head joint alone. The best note to begin with is B. The fingering diagram below will show you how to play this note.

Key to fingering diagrams
L.H. = left hand; R.H. = right-hand; Th. = left hand thumb; fingers are numbered 1 to 4 starting with the index finger.

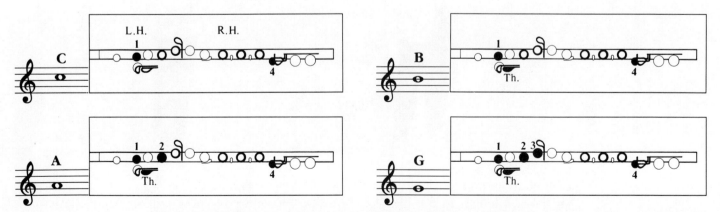

Your first week's practice should consist of ten to fifteen minutes a day—no more, no less—trying to get this B sounding as convincing as possible. For variety you may play

C, A, and G as well. This will be good preparation for your first tunes. Do not neglect this practice or feel that it must be got out of the way so you can get on to 'real music'. If you cannot sustain a steady tone on one note you will never be able to play a tune effectively.

There are so many variables which affect the flute sound that sometimes the beginner may become confused. However, all these variables can be grouped under one or other of the following three factors which are crucial to establishing a good flute sound:

Angle of the Air-Jet

This might be affected by the degree to which the head joint is rotated inwards or outwards; by tilting your head back and forth; or by the alignment of the upper and lower lip—for example a person whose upper lip protrudes significantly beyond the lower one will naturally tend to blow downwards more and needs to make allowances for this.

Speed of the Air-Jet

This is affected both by how hard you blow and by the size of the aperture between your lips.

Distance Between Lips and Embouchure Hole

This is influenced by the degree of inward rotation of the head joint; by moving the lips closer to or further away from the far edge of the embouchure hole; and by how high on your lower lip the lip-plate is positioned.

The best way to practise is to concentrate on a single one of these main factors at a time, listening carefully to your sound and noting what changes bring about improvements.

Do not be discouraged if you do not immediately succeed in producing a good sound. Learning to play with a beautiful tone is one of the greatest challenges you will ever face and it may take weeks or months of practice before you are satisfied with your sound. Below are some of the most common problems experienced by beginner flutists, and some suggestions for rectifying them:

● **Breathy sound.** While you are playing, or immediately after you have played your note, look closely at the far side of the lip-plate, just beyond the embouchure hole. There should be a small area of moisture or condensation, narrower than the embouchure hole (see Fig. 16i). If there is a large patch of condensation (Fig. 16ii) this is a sign that the hole in the centre of your lips is too wide, which will account for the breathiness of the tone. Using a mirror, check the width of the aperture between the lips, which should never be wider than the embouchure hole itself. If the area of condensation is to one side (see Fig. 16iii) this means that you are failing to centre the air-jet.

Fig. 16   i   ii   iii

Another possible explanation is that air is being wasted by being blown too far across the embouchure hole. Try to direct the air more downwards.

● **The note sounds muffled and flat.** The reason for this may be that the lips are too close to the far edge of the embouchure hole, in which case you should experiment with moving them further away; or you may be directing the air too much into the embouchure hole. Having the lip plate too high on the lower lip can also produce these symptoms.

● **The note is much too high, or suddenly jumps into the higher register.** This means that you are compressing the lips too tightly and forming too small a hole at the centre of your lips. The solution is to relax the lips a little more.

Tuning of the flute is achieved by moving the head joint in and out of the body tube, thereby decreasing or increasing the length of the instrument. If your note is too 'sharp' or high, you will need to pull the head joint out slightly—in fact this will probably be the normal position for most flutes. If the note is too 'flat' or low you will need to push the head joint in. Should you find this confusing remember that shorter tubes produce higher notes and longer tubes lower notes—think of the trumpet and tuba, or organ pipes! You should *not* fiddle with the adjuster at the top of the head joint.

If the head joint is already pushed in as far as it can go the solution to the problem may lie elsewhere: tuning can be drastically affected both by you—for example your breathing technique and embouchure—and by external factors, particularly **temperature**. When the instrument is cold it will tend to be flat. As you blow into it your breath warms the metal and the instrument rises in pitch. Significant changes in the ambient temperature will have a similarly marked effect, for example moving from a cold space to a warm space, or vice-versa.

Do not despair if you feel that you are unable to tell whether a note is in tune or not. Playing in tune is a challenge even for advanced players. Just as your brain can remember different fingering positions, so your ear can learn to discriminate tiny differences in pitch. Indeed, throughout the book you will be learning how to develop your ear as well as your technique.

TONE QUALITY

The quality of sound you produce on the flute will be greatly influenced by the quality of sound that you hear in your head. In order to develop your concept of tone quality you should listen to the great exponents of your instrument as often as possible. Here is a list of some of the most important flute players in the history of jazz.

Flute Specialists	**Saxophonists who 'Double' on Flute**
Herbie Mann	Wayman Carver
Sam Most	Frank Wess
Paul Horn	Jerome Richardson
Jeremy Steig	Bud Shank
Hubert Laws	Buddy Collette
Bob Downes	Bobby Jaspar
Chris Hinze	James Moody
James Newton	Eric Dolphy
	Sahib Shihab
	Yusef Lateef
	Roland Kirk
	Charles Lloyd
	Lew Tabackin
	Joe Farrell

Roland Kirk

Lew Tabackin

James Moody

Bud Shank

For some suggested recordings by these players please consult the discography (Appendix 2).

Listen also to the great classical flute players, like Jean-Pierre Rampal or James Galway.

It is also valuable to listen to players of other instruments whose sound you are attracted to, for example the trumpet sound of Louis Armstrong, Miles Davis or Chet Baker, or the saxophone sound of Ben Webster, Stan Getz or John Coltrane. Do not confine yourself to jazz! Remember Duke Ellington's words: 'There are only two kinds of music—good and bad.' You might improve your tone just as much by listening to a great opera singer like Jessye Norman or a great string player like Yehudi Menuhin.

Another vital foundation technique for playing the flute is tonguing. The tongue is the flute player's equivalent of a violin bow, or a drumstick. It allows you to start notes clearly and precisely, to repeat notes and to achieve all kinds of different phrasings and articulations.

Exercise 1

Imagine that you are a ventriloquist.* Sing any note that is comfortably within your voice range using the syllable 'doo'. Repeat the 'doo' sound slowly and in a steady rhythm using **one breath only**. You should produce a continuous sound as if you were singing one long note. Look at yourself in the mirror while doing this. There should be **no movement of lips, teeth or jaw**. Only the front part of the tongue moves. You will find that the tongue movements have to be very delicate to achieve this. It is also important that the tongue moves **straight up and down**.

Now you should try to apply this movement to the flute, by blowing long notes and tonguing at regular intervals, imagining the 'doo' sound and remembering to sustain the air pressure by contracting the muscles around the diaphragm. As in the 'ventriloquist' exercise the tongue makes contact with the hard palate at the roof of the mouth, just behind the top front teeth (see Fig. 17).

Do not try to tongue too rapidly—a speed of about one note every four seconds would be ideal to begin with.

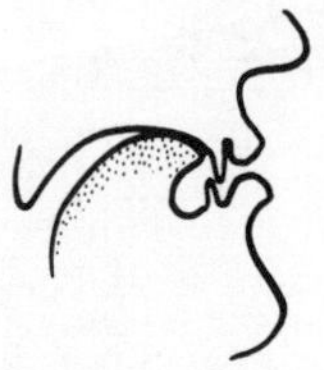

Fig. 17

* I am grateful to my first teacher Don Rendell for this exercise.

The point at which the note begins is known as the 'attack'. Up until now you have initiated the sound by allowing pressure to build up behind the lips and then 'puffing' the note out. Although this is a useful technique for producing the first sounds it is **not** how notes are usually begun. The normal procedure for starting notes involves using the tongue as a kind of valve, and should be practised as follows:

1. Breathe in.
2. Set the embouchure, with the size and shape of the aperture between the lips having been determined by your long-note practice.
3. Move the tongue up to the roof of the mouth.
4. Allow air-pressure to build up just behind the tongue. You should experience a kind of 'bottled-up' sensation, with the muscles around the diaphragm remaining firm and supporting the air-column.
5. Move the tongue down, imagining the 'doo' sound discussed above, but keeping the embouchure **absolutely still**. The note should sound immediately.

Although you will probably find it useful to practise the attack by this deliberate, stage-by-stage method, in a playing situation these five steps are performed in one rapid, flowing movement.

Stopping the Note

The note is stopped **not** by using the tongue, but rather by closing the lips, which gives a much cleaner end to the note.

During the second week you should practise long notes and then the tonguing exercises.

You have now been taught the vital foundation techniques of the flute. Whatever kind of music you play these techniques for producing and articulating the sound will always be involved, so practise them diligently.

FURTHER STUDY

Reading:

SHERIDAN W. STOKES and RICHARD A. CONDON, *Illustrated Method for Flute*. The first section of this book presents an excellent in-depth analysis, with many fine illustrations and photographs, of the foundation techniques.

Part Two:
Playing the Music

CHAPTER 1

The Staff

Music is written on a staff (plural, staves), a group of five parallel lines.

Pitch, or how high or low a note is (see under Tuning Position, p. 14) is indicated by the position of that note on the staff—the higher the note the higher it is on the staff. Music uses a seven-letter alphabet from A to G to describe the pitch of notes, but the flute range starts at C:

C   D   E   F   G   A   B   C   D   E   F   G   A

Do not worry about trying to memorize all these notes at once—you will only need to know four of them in order to play the pieces in the first two chapters.

Leger Lines

The extra lines written above and below the staff are known as leger lines.

Clefs

The sign at the beginning of the staff is a treble clef sign. The word clef is derived from the French word for a key. It shows the position of a particular note on the staff and thus is the key for finding the position of all the other notes. All flute music is written in the treble clef, a stylized form of the letter G, curling to indicate the position of that note.

Bars and Bar-Lines

Vertical lines written across the staff are bar-lines. The spaces between the bar-lines are called bars. Bars divide the music into easily recognizable units of time. They do not represent stops or pauses. They simply make counting easier, and counting, as you will see, is vital in the reading of music.

Time Signatures

If you look at the beginning of 'Blues for Beginners' you will see two numbers written one over the other. This is the time signature. It can be thought of as a fraction, the top figure or numerator telling us the number of beats in the bar and the bottom figure or denominator the kind of beat. In this case there are four **quarter** or **crotchet** beats in each bar.

Note Durations

The table below shows the note durations that you will encounter in your first pieces and exercises:

Symbol	British Term	American Term	Number of Beats to Count in 4/4 Time
♩ or ♪	Crotchet	Quarter Note	One
♩ or ♪	Minim	Half Note	Two
o	Semibreve	Whole Note	Four

Pulse and Rhythm

Look at 'Blues for Beginners'. Count in groups of four beats and clap on every first beat, holding the hands together to express the duration of the semibreve,* which is four beats.

```
clap:   x            x            x            x
count:  1  2  3  4   1  2  3  4   1  2  3  4   1  2  3  4, etc.
```

What you are doing is counting the **pulse** and clapping the **rhythm**.

Rhythm is the organization of notes in time and is not **necessarily** regular, although in this instance it is. Pulse—often referred to as 'the beat'—is usually felt rather than heard and is nearly always regular. It is very often what we dance to in music. Pulse determines the speed of the music and helps us to measure the distance between notes.

Now you should practise counting and clapping with the CD accompaniment to 'Blues for Beginners'. The claps should coincide precisely with the notes of the flute. This procedure of counting and clapping before playing should be carefully adhered to throughout the book. Rhythm is the most basic element of music, and it is vital to master this aspect of each piece before proceeding further.

Taking a Breath

The commas written above the stave are suggested breathing places. Breaths should not be taken where doing so would destroy the flow of the music. There is a parallel here with speech, where breaths are generally taken at the end of sentences or phrases, except by small children who are still learning the art!

In 'Blues for Beginners' there are no spaces between the notes. In such cases you must create a breathing space by cutting the note before the breath mark slightly short. You should take small sips of air at regular intervals. Most beginners drastically overestimate the amount of breath they need—small amounts will be sufficient provided that the breath is adequately supported by the muscles around the diaphragm. Inhale through the mouth, trying to disturb your embouchure as little as possible. **Do not breathe through your nose!**

The following exercise may help you to become accustomed to the correct mode of breathing. Breathe at the commas. The rhythm should be regular and undisturbed by the taking of the breath. Count slowly and steadily.

Count aloud: 1 2 3 4 1 2 3 4 ' 1 2 3 4 1 2 3 4 ', etc.

Metronome Markings

Now you are ready to play 'Blues for Beginners'. The instruction ♩ = 100 at the beginning of the piece is a metronome marking, meaning that the music is to be played at a

---

* Claps can only indicate the position of notes in time—not their duration.

speed of around 100 beats per minute. A metronome is a device which marks the pulse by means of a regular click and would be a worthwhile purchase (see Appendix 3). Fingering positions for the pieces in this chapter and the following one are shown in the diagrams on p. 12.

Blues for Beginners[**]

Rests

'A la Mode' and 'Progression' introduce minims, and minim and semibreve rests. A minim is worth two beats in 4/4 time. The minim rest sits on the third line, measuring from the bottom of the staff upwards, and represents two beats of silence, while the semibreve rest hangs from the fourth line, representing four beats of silence. Silence in music is just as important as sound, so make sure you count the rests carefully.

There is an optional harmony part to 'A la Mode', which can be played by a teacher or more advanced player.

A la Mode

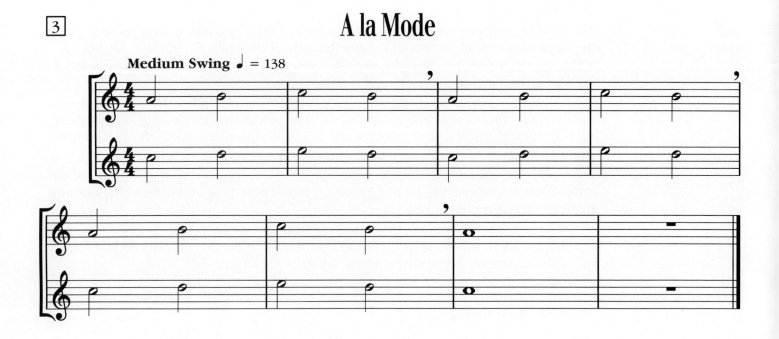

[*] The numbers refer to tracks on the CD.
[**] All pieces are by John O'Neill unless otherwise indicated.

Repeats

At the end of 'Progression' is a double bar preceded by two dots. This means that you repeat from the beginning. There is only one repeat unless otherwise indicated.

4

Progression

CHAPTER

2

Riffs

'Out for the Count' (overleaf) is a twelve-bar blues consisting of a single phrase which is repeated three times. Short repeated phrases of this type are know as riffs. They were often used by big bands during the swing era as a means of building excitement, with different riffs sometimes being assigned to each section of the band. The Count Basie Band of the 1930s is a perfect example.

Frank Foster with the Count Basie Band

Crotchets

This is the first piece to use crotchets, which are worth one beat each in 4/4 time.

The 'Pick-Up'

You will notice that there are just two crotchets before the first bar-line, in spite of the fact that the time signature indicates four beats to each bar. These two crotchets are an example of an **anacrusis**, sometimes referred to by jazz musicians as a '**pick-up**'. An anacrusis is an unstressed note or group of notes at the beginning of a musical phrase. In this instance, the first strong accent falls on the C and not the G or A. Because of the anacrusis, there is only a two-beat rest in the bar before the repeat.

Out for the Count

⑤

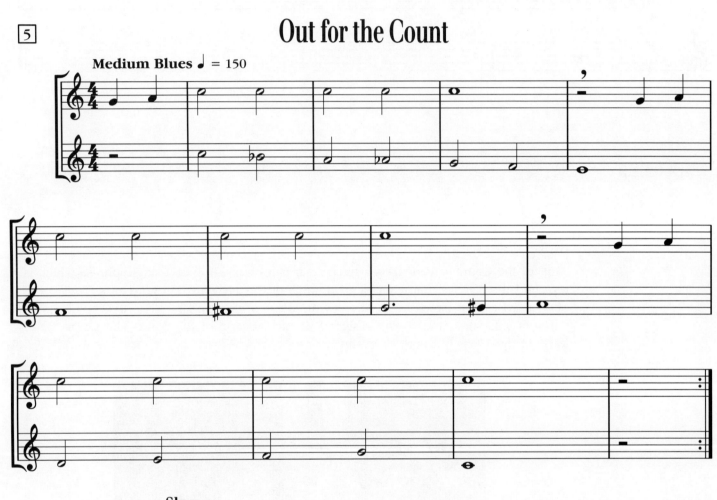

Slurs

The curved lines above the notes are **slurs**. You should tongue only the first note within a slur group. For example, in the first bar of the following piece you tongue only the first B.

Times Remembered

⑥

P.M.

Third Attempt

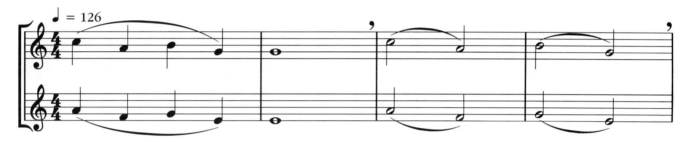

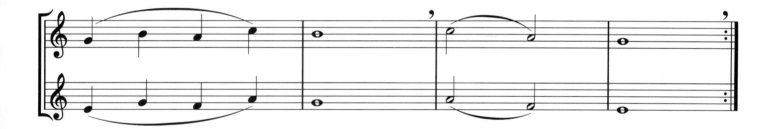

FURTHER STUDY

Listening:

COUNT BASIE, 'Jumping at the Woodside' from *Swinging the Blues*. A classic example of the use of riffs.

CHAPTER 3

The four tunes in this section contain two new notes—low F and E.

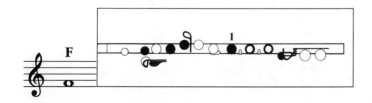

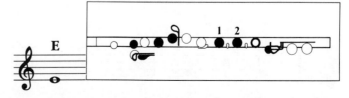

Dynamic Markings

The pieces in this chapter contain **dynamic markings**. These are abbreviations of Italian words and are used to indicate volume levels. Here are some of those most commonly used:

Marking	Italian word	Meaning
pp	*pianissimo*	very quiet
p	*piano*	quiet
mp	*mezzopiano*	medium quiet
mf	*mezzoforte*	medium loud
f	*forte*	loud
ff	*fortissimo*	very loud

Changes in volume on the flute are achieved by varying two factors—the degree of contraction of the muscles around the diaphragm and the size of the aperture between the lips.

When playing quietly you need to contract the muscles more firmly and decrease the size of the aperture; when playing loudly the muscles relax a little more to expel the air from the body more quickly and the aperture increases in size.

The following exercise is excellent for practising control of dynamics. Try to make sure that each note begins and ends at the same volume and that you achieve six distinct dynamic levels. You can play this exercise using any of the notes you have learnt so far.

The Pause

The sign ⌒ is a **pause**, sometimes called a *fermata*, which means the note should be extended beyond its written value, at the discretion of the performer or musical director. In the exercise you should therefore pause on each note and take a new breath before you play the next one.

Crotchet Rests

The sign 𝄾 in 'Flat 5' is a crotchet or quarter-note rest. It represents one beat of silence in 4/4 time.

Ties

In 'Flat 5' you will notice that the last two notes are connected by a curved line. This is called a **tie**. It has the effect of joining the two notes together as one, so you do not tongue the second G, but simply extend it by four extra beats. Do not confuse ties with slurs. A tie always connects notes of the same pitch, whereas a slur connects notes of different pitch.

9

Flat 5

Interstellar

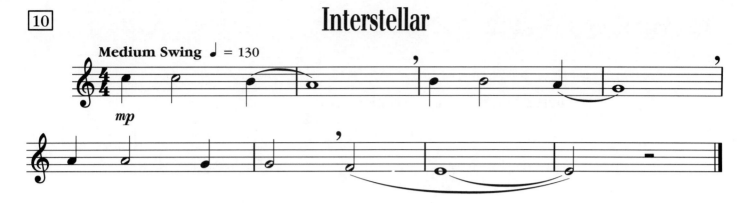

Syncopation

'251' is made more difficult by the presence of **syncopation**, which can be defined as the placing of accents where you would not normally expect to find them—the effect being one of rhythmic surprise. Much of the vitality of jazz derives from the extensive use of syncopated rhythms. In this example it is the fourth beats of the first, third and fifth bars which are syncopated.

251

In 'Home Bass' you will notice after the first two crotchets a double bar with dots placed **after** it. This is an indication of where you repeat **from**.

The dynamic marking **mp-f** means you should play mezzopiano the first time and forte on the repeat.

Home Bass

FURTHER STUDY

It is important that you spend some of your practice time playing by ear. Try to memorize some of the tunes you have learnt so far and play them without the music. Inventing your own tunes would also be a good idea.

Play the lower part of 'Third Attempt' from the previous chapter.

Sharps, Semitones and Accidentals

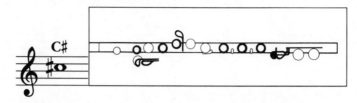

In 'James' you will find middle C♯ for the first time. This note is indicated by a **sharp** sign written in front of the C. A sharp means the note is raised by one **semitone**, which is the distance between one note and its nearest neighbour note, and the smallest interval that is 'officially' recognized in the mainstream of Western music. Signs which alter notes in this way are called **accidentals**. Accidentals affect every note of the same pitch in the bar, so in bar 3 of 'James' **both** C's are sharp.

This tune is an example of the bossa-nova rhythm, made famous in jazz by the early sixties recordings of tenor saxophonist Stan Getz.

Dotted Notes

The first note is a minim with a dot placed after it. A dot placed after a note extends its duration by half as much again. A dotted minim is therefore worth three beats (2 + 1).

13

James

'South View' introduces F♯. The sign ▬▬ at the beginning of the piece means that you remain silent for eight bars. Count carefully so that you know exactly when to come in.

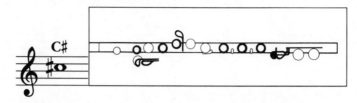

South View

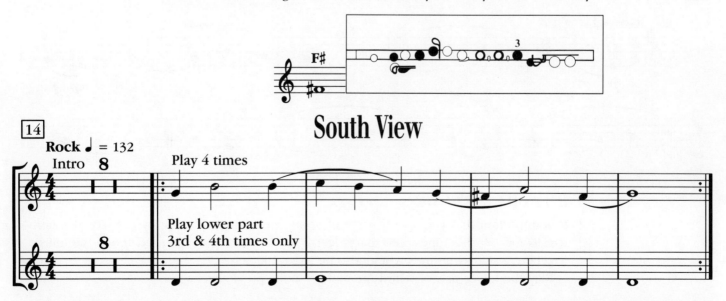

The Natural Sign

In 'Minor Problem' the second note of bars 1, 3 and 5 is preceded by another kind of accidental, the **natural** sign ♮, which cancels any previous accidentals in the bar.

15

Minor Problem

Medium Groove ♩ = 130

FURTHER STUDY

Listening:

STAN GETZ, *Jazz Samba; Stan Getz and Joao Gilberto.* Both of these records are classic examples of the use of the bossa-nova rhythm in jazz.

Stan Getz

CHAPTER 5

The pieces in this chapter introduce B♭. The flat sign is another accidental, meaning that the note placed after it is to be played a semitone **lower.**

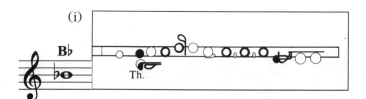 (i)

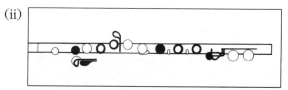 (ii)

As you will see from the diagrams there are two ways of fingering this note. One of the advantages of thumb B♭ (i) is that the thumb may remain in position on this key while playing any notes that involve depressing the second finger of the left hand, in other words from A down to low E. For example, when moving from A to B♭, as in the third bar of 'Roberto', the thumb may remain on the B♭ key. Thumb B♭ may therefore be regarded as your first choice fingering for any piece or passage, like 'Roberto', in which all the B's are flat.

However, when you have to alternate between B♭ and B natural, as in the first line of 'Delta City' or the whole of 'Gangsterland', you should use the 'long' fingering (ii), since the thumb B♭ is rather awkward in such situations. You may also find the long B♭ useful when moving between B♭ and F, as in the sixth bar of 'Delta City'.

Key Signatures

When accidentals are placed in between the clef sign and the time signature as in 'Roberto' they form a **key signature**, which tells you which notes are to be played sharp or flat for the duration of the entire piece rather than just for a single bar. In this case the placement of the flat sign on the middle line of the stave means that all B's are to be played flat unless otherwise indicated by an accidental.

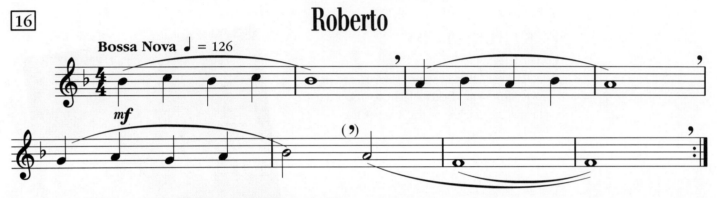

Enharmonic Notes

'Delta City' introduces D♭, which is another name for the note C♯. The note in between C and D is both one semitone higher than C (C♯) and one semitone lower than D (D♭). Notes like C♯ and D♭ which can be named in two ways are said to be **enharmonic notes.** It is essential that you learn to think of these notes in both ways.

First and Second Time Bars

This piece also introduces **first and second time bars.** These are frequently used to save space on repeats. The second time bars are played as an **alternative**—never in addition—to the first time bars on the repeat.

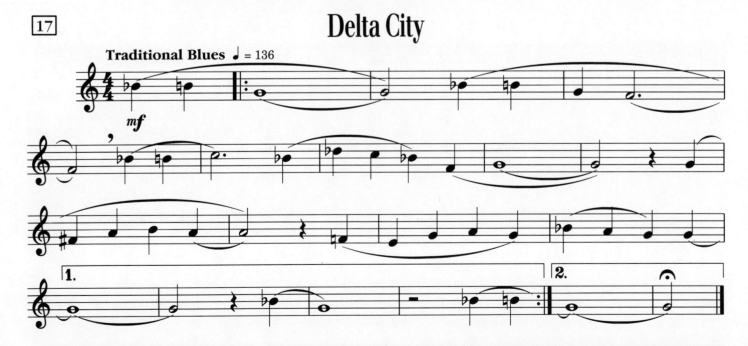

Crescendo and Decrescendo

When it is wished to indicate that the music should gradually get louder or softer this can be done in two ways: either by writing *cresc.* or *decresc.*— (Italian = *crescendo* or *decrescendo*, meaning getting louder or softer); or by the signs ──── and ────. To practise this try the following exercise, using other notes for variation. Listen carefully to ensure that you keep the pitch steady.

Accents

'Gangsterland' introduces **accents**. The sign ∧ over the first note is a short accent, meaning that the note is to be attacked hard and then stopped short of its full written value.* The sign > over the second note means that the beginning of the note should be played with extra emphasis. This is achieved by a slight 'kick' of the diaphragm, similar to what happens when you cough.

Gangsterland

---

* Note for teachers: this is **not** the same as the classical staccato, which is lighter and shorter.

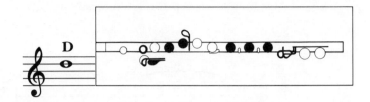

The Break

One of the major technical problems of the flute is crossing the 'break', or moving to middle register D from the notes below. This involves considerable finger coordination and the exercise below will be a useful preparatory study.

Play the exercise slowly and evenly, with good tone, slurring throughout, with the exception of the initial attack note.

Do not be discouraged if you are not immediately successful at crossing the break. It is a technical challenge even for more advanced players.

'Breaking Point' will provide similar technical practice with CD accompaniment.

Breaking Point

19

'Transition' introduces E above the break. The fingering position for this note is exactly the same as for the E in the lower register (see fingering diagram on p.23). Whether you produce the higher or lower note depends firstly on the sound you hear in your head and secondly on subtle changes in the embouchure. In order to produce higher notes the following adjustments to the embouchure are necessary:

● The aperture between the lips should be smaller.
● Your lower lip should cover more of the embouchure hole (somewhere between a third and a half).
● The lips must move closer to the far edge of the embouchure hole.
● The air-stream will need to be directed more downwards.

The best means of experiencing what is required is to practise **daily**, as part of your warm up, the following exercise. It is very important that the exercise be played **slurred.** Try to imagine the sound of the second note before you play it and listen carefully to ensure that the two notes are in tune:

Transition

Sylvie's Dance

'K.O.' (overleaf) introduces low D. Notice that the fingering position is slightly different from that of middle D—the index finger of the left hand also has to be depressed.

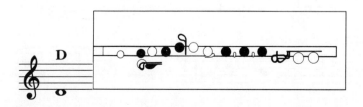

K.O.

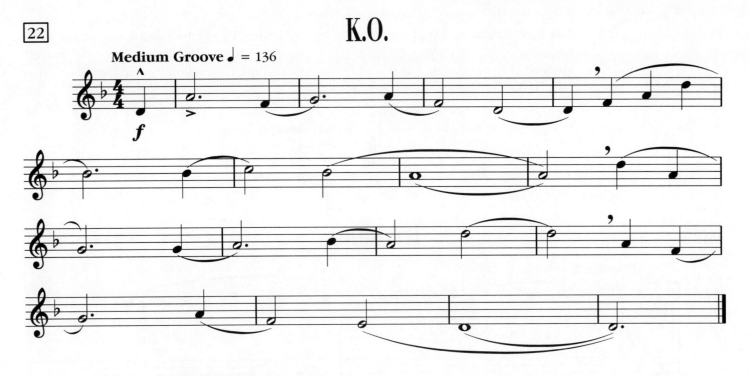

FURTHER STUDY

Playing:

Play the lower part of 'A la Mode' from Chapter 1, and the lower part of 'South View' from Chapter 4.

CHAPTER 7

See fingering diagrams on pp. 23 and 12 respectively.

'Blue Jean' introduces F and G above the break. Your daily practice of octaves (see previous chapter) should now be extended to include these notes as well. Keep the throat open and relaxed and remember to support the air column by contracting the muscles around the diaphragm. Try to achieve the feeling of your sound 'floating on air'.

Blue Jean

Improvisation

After you have played the tune of 'Blue Jean' try improvising with the accompaniment, using the following five notes:

It would be a good idea to learn these notes by heart before attempting to improvise.

During this improvised section you may play whatever you feel using these notes only. You can play the notes in any register, so you can also play low G, and E and D. You need not worry about playing any 'wrong' notes, since all of these notes will sound fine wherever you play them.

Most beginner improvisers make the mistake of neglecting the rhythmic aspect of their playing. The following exercises should help with this problem:

- Clap out a solo, or tap one out on your legs or on a table top. Be as adventurous as you like, but try to maintain a strong rhythmic feeling in what you do, like a good jazz drummer.
- Once you are happy about clapping a solo return to the flute and try improvising again, using **only the note A** and trying to retain the strong rhythmic feeling you had while you were clapping.
- Once you feel comfortable improvising with a single note add the C, and try to play a solo using just two notes.
- In a similar fashion add the remaining notes, **one at a time**, always focusing on rhythm. It may be helpful to think of the scale as a set of 'tuned drums', with your tongue as the 'drumstick'.

These exercises should have helped you to realize that **the most important element of any jazz solo is rhythm.**

The following exercises will give you additional valuable practise at crossing the break. Play them slowly, gradually increasing the tempo.

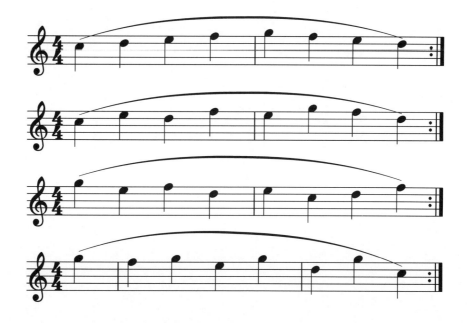

N.B. The second and third exercises can be played as a duet.

Scales

The word scale is derived from the Italian *scala*—'staircase' or 'ladder'. It is a series of single notes moving up or down in steps.

Chords

A **chord** is a combination of notes sounding together. Simple three-note chords are known as **triads**.

It is impossible to play chords on the flute in the way that a keyboard player or guitarist can, although some players have experimented with **multiphonics**—the playing of more than one note by use of alternative fingerings and advanced blowing techniques.

Arpeggios

An arpeggio is a chord played **melodically**, sounding the notes one after the other, rather than **harmonically**, playing the notes simultaneously.

Scales and arpeggios are the 'nuts and bolts' of most jazz improvisation, although to achieve good results creative rather than mechanical use must be made of them!

Below are the scales and arpeggio of F major and D minor. You will notice that they share the same key signature. They are known as relative keys. They contain the same notes, except the seventh note of the D minor scale is sharpened, shown by an accidental and not in the key signature. There are various forms of the minor scale, this particular one being known as the harmonic minor.*

The scales and arpeggios should be committed to memory and played slowly, gradually increasing the speed as your technique develops. Strive for rhythmic and tonal evenness. Scales and arpeggios should initially be played slurred to develop smooth technique. Once this has been mastered they may be tongued as well.

---

* The construction of major and minor scales and arpeggios will be discussed at greater length in Chapter 17, p. 60.

D harmonic minor scale

D minor arpeggio

Once you are feeling comfortable with the F major scale and arpeggio try playing them with track 24 on the CD. When you can manage this you should begin to improvise using the scale notes.

CHAPTER

'Devil Music' and 'Bird Waltz' introduce G♯/A♭ and D♯/E♭, both of which are further examples of enharmonic notes.

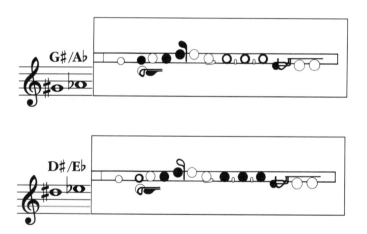

Both notes involve coordination of the two weakest fingers. The fingering exercises below are designed to strengthen them and should be incorporated into your warm-up until you have mastered them. Play them slowly at first (♩ = 60), gradually increasing the tempo.

The line written above and below the notes in bars 9 and 10 of 'Devil Music' are **tenuto** marks, meaning that these notes should be held for their full value and connected as smoothly as possible.

Devil Music

'Bird Waltz' is a blues inspired by the music of Charlie Parker (1920–1955), sometimes known as Bird. He was one of the greatest ever jazz musicians and together with Dizzy Gillespie, Bud Powell and others created Bebop, a jazz style which dominated the 1940s, and has continued to exert a powerful influence on contemporary music.

3/4 Time

This tune introduces 3/4 or waltz time, in which there are three crotchet beats to each bar. 3/4 time was rarely heard in jazz before the 1950s. It has become much more popular since then, and is particularly associated with the music of the lyrical and highly influential pianist Bill Evans.

Transposition

I have written 'Bird Waltz' in two keys, C and B major. The process of moving a tune into a different key is known as **transposition**. Transposition is one of the most effective ways of improving your knowledge of keys, getting to know your instrument and training your ear.

The note G♭ in bar 8 is enharmonically equivalent to F♯.

Bird Waltz (C Major)

F#/Gb

See fingering diagram on p. 26.

See fingering diagram on p. 26.

27

Bird Waltz (B Major)

Jazz Waltz ♩ = 132

You may recognize the scale at the end of 'A Song for Sophie' (see p. 38) as the same five-note scale with which you improvised over the backing track of 'Blue Jean', but this time starting on D instead of A. This is a **pentatonic scale** sometimes referred to as the **minor pentatonic.** The sign 𝄍 indicates a whole-bar repeat.

From this tune onwards detailed indications of where to tongue (articulation markings) have been omitted. You should experiment with many different possibilities for phrasing and expression, marking them in your copy with a soft pencil so that they can easily be altered. The following points may help to guide you:

- The first note of any new phrase should nearly always be tongued.
- Tongue only those notes which require extra emphasis.
- Avoid 'phrasing to the bar-line' or tonguing the first beat of every bar. This kind of phrasing is particularly inappropriate to jazz.
- How to articulate a passage is often a matter of individual taste. There is more than one 'right' way.
- You will learn a lot by listening carefully to the example on the CD and to the recordings of great jazz players. Jazz is a language that is often best learnt by imitation.

A

See fingering diagram on p. 12.

See fingering diagram on p. 12.

A Song for Sophie

Medium ♩ = 126

Use of Space

Make sure you do not clutter your solos with too many notes. The best jazz musicians know how to make effective use of **space**. There are two ways of creating space in a solo—one is by using silence and the other is by playing notes of longer duration. In either case you will find you have more time to be aware of what you and—just as importantly—the other musicians are doing. As a result your playing should become more relaxed, expressive and coherent. Trumpeter Miles Davis is a fine example of someone who uses space quite brilliantly.

Chromatic Scale

Now that you have learnt G♯/A♭ and low D♯/E♭ you are able to practise the **chromatic scale**, in which one moves by semitone steps from any note to the same note in the next register. The example below shows a chromatic scale starting on F. In order to give you more practice with enharmonic notes I have written sharps in the ascending version and flats in the descending version of the scale.

FURTHER STUDY

Playing:

As an exercise in transposition try playing any of the tunes you have played so far starting on a different note. Other good material for transposition would be simple folk tunes or nursery rhymes.

Listening:

CHARLIE PARKER, 'Blues for Alice' from *Charles Parker*.

BILL EVANS, 'Waltz for Debbie', from *At the Village Vanguard*. A beautiful example of a jazz waltz.

MILES DAVIS, *Kind of Blue*. Listen in particular to the trumpet solos for examples of the use of space.

Reading:

ROSS RUSSELL, *Bird Lives*.

GARY GIDDINS, *Celebrating Bird: The Triumph of Charlie Parker*.

ROBERT REISNER, *Bird: The Legend of Charlie Parker*.

Viewing:

'Bird' directed by Clint Eastwood.

Miles Davis

CHAPTER

10

Sight-reading is only one of the many skills a good jazz musician must acquire. A discriminating ear is one of the most vital assets, since effective improvisation depends on being able to translate the ideas in your head on to the instrument as quickly as possible.

Ear Training

A lucky minority seem to develop fantastic aural perception at a very early age. At the other end of the spectrum true 'tone-deafness' is much rarer than people imagine. For the vast majority in between these extremes aural training can produce remarkable results.

Intervals

One important skill is the ability to recognize and sing **intervals.** Intervals are a means of expressing the distance between one note and another. You should begin to develop your sense of this by learning to sing the intervals of the major and minor scales. The chart below indicates the names of these intervals in the D major scale, measuring them from the first note, also known as the **tonic**. The degrees of the scale are expressed as Roman numerals:

Major scale (D)

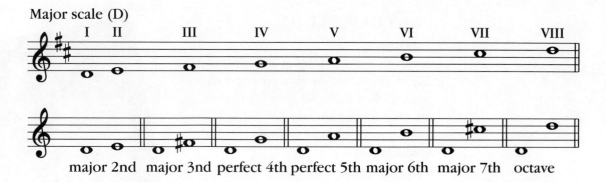

major 2nd   major 3nd   perfect 4th   perfect 5th   major 6th   major 7th   octave

The intervals between successive degrees of the harmonic minor scale and the tonic are the same, except I-III (which is a minor third) and I-VI (a minor sixth); these two intervals are a semitone smaller than their major counterparts:

Harmonic Minor Scale (D)

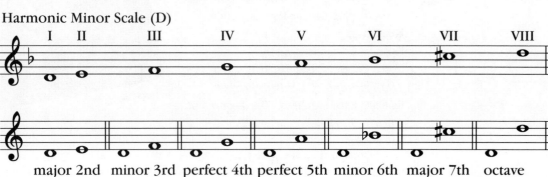

major 2nd   minor 3rd   perfect 4th   perfect 5th   minor 6th   major 7th   octave

It is important to realize that the intervals are the same for every key. Thus, the distance between the tonic and the fifth note of any major or minor scale, measured as an ascending interval, is always a perfect fifth.

In the exercises which follow try not to be too self-conscious about your singing. Accuracy of pitch is more important than tone quality. Singing will help your flute playing and vice-versa—the technique of supporting the breath and relaxing the throat is almost identical.

Some intervals are much harder to sing than others. It is best to begin with trying to recognize and sing the ascending intervals.

Exercises for singing intervals

It would be an advantage to do this exercise at a keyboard. You would then be able to hear what the two notes sound like when played together.

  (i)   Play slowly from D to the A above a few times to establish the sound of the interval in your head.
  (ii) Play D.
  (iii) Imagine the sound of the A.
  (iv) Sing A.

Should you find it difficult to pitch this interval sing up the steps of the scale until you reach the required note. The next stage is to imagine singing up to the note without actually vocalizing. Once this is mastered it will not be long before you can find the correct pitch without singing the notes in between.

You should work towards being able to sing the interval without the preparatory step (i), and in as many different keys as possible. Do not be surprised if it takes you several days or weeks to master a particular interval.

Once you are confident with fifths you can progress to other intervals. A recommended order of study is: perfect fifth, perfect fourth, octave, major second, major third, minor third, major sixth, minor sixth, major seventh.

Some students find it helpful to use mnemonics for the intervals. For example, the first two notes of 'Oh When the Saints Go Marching In' are a major third apart. Some other possibly helpful mnemonics are 'Here Comes the Bride' for a perfect fourth, 'Twinkle Twinkle Little Star' for a perfect fifth and 'My Bonny Lies Over the Ocean' for a major sixth. You might wish to substitute some tunes of your own—the more familiar the better.

Having developed an ability to sing ascending intervals, you should next practise descending intervals. These are named in the major and harmonic minor scales as follows:

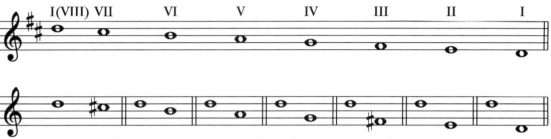

minor 2nd   minor 3rd   perfect 4th   perfect 5th   minor 6th   minor 7th   octave

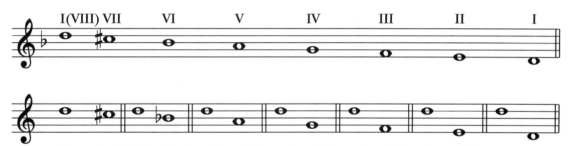

minor 2nd   major 3rd   perfect 4th   perfect 5th   major 6th   minor 7th   octave

Inversions

The interval which measures the distance between the same pair of named notes but in the opposite direction, e.g., from D **down** to E rather than **up** to E, is known as an **inversion**. The original interval and its inversion always add up to nine, e.g., seconds become sevenths and fourths become fifths; major intervals become minor when inverted and minor intervals become major; perfect intervals remain perfect.

You should practise singing descending intervals by adapting the exercises given above. A suggested order of study is: perfect fourth, octave, minor third, minor second, perfect fifth, major third, minor sixth, major sixth, minor seventh.

Playing by Ear

Playing by ear is one of the most enjoyable and effective ways of improving your aural perception. Any material will do—nursery rhymes, hymns, folk tunes, songs you hear on the radio, T.V. themes, advertising jingles—but the most relevant exercise would be to get hold of jazz recordings and learn to play jazz tunes. You will also develop your sound, sense of time and phrasing by listening to the jazz masters in this way.

If you cannot afford to buy the records, visit your local music library, which will often contain an excellent record collection. This is a good way to become familiar with the jazz heritage. You should start with simple melodies. Recordings by singers, for example the 1950s recordings of Frank Sinatra, are also good source material.

Proceed as follows:

1. Play the recording several times.
2. Sing the melody with the recording, trying to imitate as closely as possible with your voice the inflections of the instrument or voice. This technique of imitating instrumental sounds with the voice is known as **scat-singing.** Louis Armstrong, Ella Fitzgerald, Chet Baker, Al Jarreau and Bobby McFerrin are five of the very best scat-singers.
3. Sing the melody without the recording—this is much harder!
4. Play the melody with the recording. This will develop the ability to translate what you hear in your head to your fingers—a vital skill for musicians who wish to improvise.
5. Play the melody without the recording.

You may find this difficult at first but please persevere—it becomes easier with practice. This sort of exercise will develop your playing considerably.

Later on you can progress to more intricate melodies and even jazz solos. Some sort of device for slowing the music down to half-speed is invaluable. This could be either a reel-to-reel tape-recorder which records at both $7^1/2$ and $3^3/4$ ips or a record player which slows down to 16 rpm, preferably with sliding pitch control to facilitate tuning. Cassette players with slow-down facility are also available. These items can be relatively cheaply acquired through small-ad pages of newspapers, junk shops or second-hand audio equipment shops. The ability to slow down solos opens up a whole world of difficult music to your ears. Charlie Parker is said to have used this method to study the music of his idol Lester Young.

FURTHER STUDY

Playing:

This game can be played with your teacher or another flute player: position yourselves so that neither player can see the other's fingerings, and take it in turns to sound any note. The other player must try to sound the same note in response. By practising regularly at this game you will be surprised how easy it becomes to find the correct note on the first attempt.

Reading:

PAUL HINDEMITH, *Elementary Training for Musicians*.
Not for the faint-hearted! This book contains at least two years' study. But well worth the effort.

Listening:

LOUIS ARMSTRONG, 'Basin Street Blues' from *Hot 5 and Hot 7*.

ELLA FITZGERALD, 'Rockin' in Rhythm' from *Sings the Duke Ellington Songbook*.

CHET BAKER, 'But Not For Me' from *The Touch of Your Lips*.

AL JARREAU, 'Roof Garden' and 'Blue Rondo a la Turk' from *Breakin' Away*.

BOBBY McFERRIN, 'Walkin'' from *Spontaneous Inventions*.

The above recordings are all examples of scat-singing.

Louis Armstrong

11

Even Quavers

In classical music quavers, or eighth notes, are invariably given half the value of crotchets but in jazz they can be interpreted in different ways. This chapter will deal with the classical interpretation, sometimes referred to by jazz musicians as 'even quavers' or 'straight eighths'.

Single quavers are written thus

Beams

When there are two or more quavers they may be connected by a beam, e.g.

Perform the following exercises:

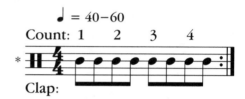

Quavers can also be counted in this way:

To perform the drumming exercise below sit on a chair with your feet on the floor and the palms of your hands resting on the top of your thighs. You should attempt it very slowly at first.

These notes are introduced in the following two pieces:

See fingering diagrams on pp. 27, 35 and 12 respectively.

The House in the Forest

[29]

'Tongue-Twister' is an exercise for rapid tonguing, but do not strive for speed at the expense of even tone and rhythm. It is better to begin slowly and gradually increase the tempo, using a metronome if one is available.

Tongue-Twister

[30]

'Lullaby' is an example of a tune in a **jazz-rock** style. This style always calls for an even-quaver interpretation.

If you experience problems with the tied rhythms, e.g. in bars 2 and 4, try playing the phrase first **without the tie**. This will help you to hear the correct placement of the notes.

D.C. al Fine

The direction **D.C. al Fine** is short for **Da Capo al Fine** (literally 'from the beginning to the end') and means repeat from the start of the piece and stop at the word *Fine*.

Rallentando

Rall. is an abbreviation of *rallentando*, meaning 'getting slower'.

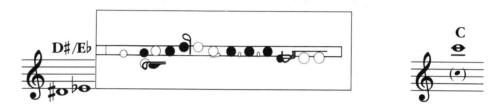

See fingering diagram on p. 12.

Lullaby

Ted Gioia

Scale and arpeggio practice: C major

A minor

FURTHER STUDY

Listening:
TED GIOIA, 'Lullaby in G' from *The End of the Open Road.*

Playing:
Extend your practice of octaves to the new notes you have learnt in this chapter.

CHAPTER   12

Triplet Quavers

Triplet quavers occur when a crotchet beat is subdivided into three. They are notated like this:

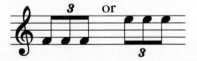

Perform the following exercise:

One way of counting this rhythm is:

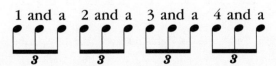

Drumming exercise

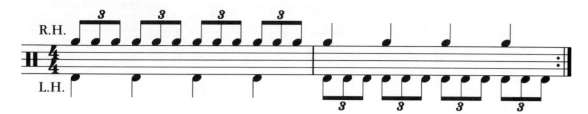

This exercise for rhythm and articulation would make an ideal daily warm-up, and should be practised on different notes throughout the flute range:

Moon Tune

32

Ballad ♩ = 54

'The Loneliest Monk' (overleaf) is dedicated to the late Thelonious Monk (1917–82), a pianist and composer whose extraordinary originality was coupled with a wry humour.

Thelonious Monk

C#/Db

See fingering diagram on p. 26.

The Loneliest Monk

33

Slow blues ♩ = 86

Scale and arpeggio practice: G major

Improvise in G major using track 34 on the CD.

E minor

FURTHER STUDY

Listening:

THELONIOUS MONK, *The Composer*

This chapter deals with quavers which are played with a 'swing' rather than with even interpretation.

Swing Quavers

It is important to understand that there is no **visual** distinction between swing (or 'jazz') quavers and even quavers. The notes are written the same way but interpreted differently, the on-beat quaver having a value of two thirds of a beat and the off-beat quaver one third of a beat. Swing quavers are therefore closely related to triplet quavers:

but to notate them as they are played would be untidy and unnecessarily complicated.

Practise the following exercise:

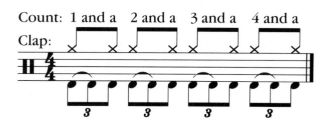

Scat-singing (see Chapter 10, p. 42) is an excellent way of establishing the correct 'feel' for jazz rhythms. One way of scatting jazz quavers is:

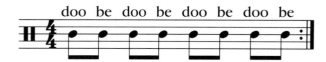

There are many other possibilities. Try inventing your own sounds. When the off-beat quaver is followed by silence, as in 'Trane Refrain' I prefer a more emphatic scat-sound:

To Swing Or Not To Swing?

You may be wondering how you are to know whether the quavers should be played 'straight' or 'swung'. In many cases this is indicated by the expression markings at the beginning of the piece. Sometimes the composer/arranger specifically requests the desired quaver interpretation. In other cases the idiom dictates what is required. For example, if the piece is marked 'jazz-rock', 'latin', 'bossa-nova' or 'calypso' the quavers are played even, but 'swing', or 'medium blues' indicates jazz quavers.* If in doubt, try both ways and make an artistic choice!

With jazz quavers a little extra emphasis is generally given to the off-beat quaver. To achieve this jazz musicians often slur from off-beat to on-beat. Tonguing all the on-beats can make the music sound laboured. In order to practise this kind of phrasing scales should be played as follows:

* At fast tempos, even in music in a swing idiom, the quavers are played straight, since a smooth swing interpretation is impossible to achieve.

You should also practise tonguing on every other off-beat quaver:

D.S. al Coda

The term *D.S. al Coda*, an abbreviation of *Dal Segno al Coda*, means literally 'from the sign to the tail'. A coda is an extra section which is added to a piece. When you meet this instruction you repeat from the sign 𝄋 and then go to the coda at the coda sign ⊕.

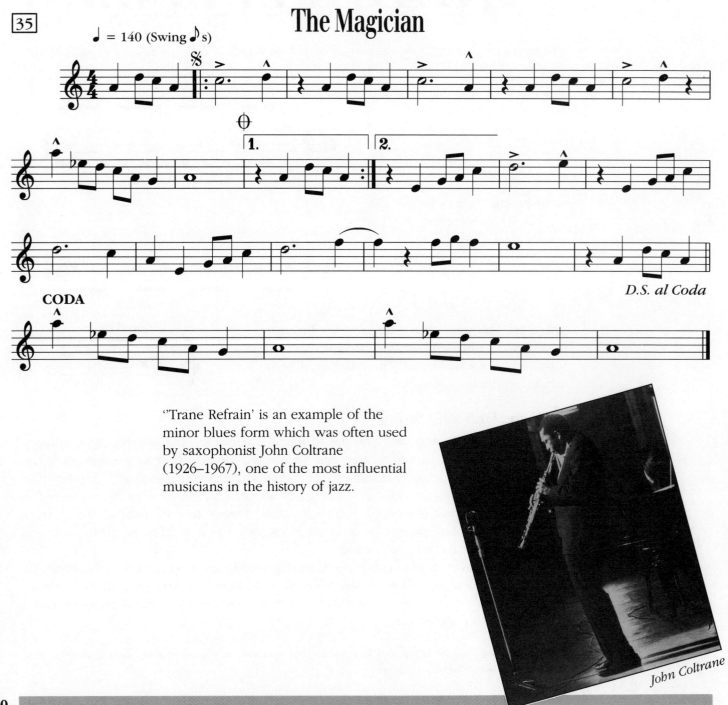

''Trane Refrain' is an example of the minor blues form which was often used by saxophonist John Coltrane (1926–1967), one of the most influential musicians in the history of jazz.

John Coltrane

Anticipation

When an off-beat quaver is followed by a rest, as in the first six bars, or when it is tied over, as in the final six bars, it is often easier **not** to count the on-beat which immediately follows. This is because the off-beat quaver functions as an **anticipation** of the following beat. It can therefore feel rushed and uncomfortable to count the next beat, especially if the tempo is fast. Try to 'feel' this beat without consciously counting it.

"Trane Refrain

'Blue Monk' is one of Thelonious Monk's most celebrated compositions.

The Blues Scale/Passing Notes

In 'Blue Monk' there is a twelve-bar improvisation section. The suggested scale for improvisation is often referred to by jazz educators as the **blues scale.** It is similar to the minor pentatonic scales you used for 'Blue Jean' in Chapter 7 and 'Song for Sophie' in Chapter 9 but it has one extra note—the flattened fifth, which in this case is F♭ (enharmonically equivalent to E natural). This note has a very strong blues feeling. It sounds extremely **dissonant** or restless when played by itself and is more often used by jazz musicians as a **passing note**, or connecting note, as in bars 1 and 3 of the upper part.

Blue Monk

Thelonious Monk

© 1962, Bocu Music Ltd. All rights reserved. Used by permission

Repetition

A key word to remember when improvising is **repetition**. Many beginner improvisers make the mistake of simply running up and down the scale rather aimlessly. Repetition of single notes in interesting rhythms is a good way of breaking this habit. Saxophonists Lester Young and Sonny Rollins provide masterly examples of how effective note repetition can be in a jazz solo. Equally important is the use of riffs (see Chapter 2, p. 21), for which you will find no better model than guitarist Charlie Christian. Experiment by inventing your own riffs on 'Blue Monk' using the given scale.

FURTHER STUDY

Listening:

JOHN COLTRANE, 'Mr P.C.' from *Giant Steps* as an example of a minor blues.
THELONIOUS MONK, 'Blue Monk' from *The Composer*.
CHARLIE CHRISTIAN, *The Genius of the Electric Guitar*.

CHAPTER 14

Off-Beat Phrases

So far all the phrases which you have played have started on the beat. The pieces in this chapter feature phrases which begin **off** the beat.

To begin with you may find it helpful to indicate the position of every quaver by counting as follows:

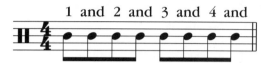

When you play phrases which begin off the beat you will therefore be entering on the 'and'. The example below shows how this counting method could be applied to the first two bars of 'A Bossa for Betty'.

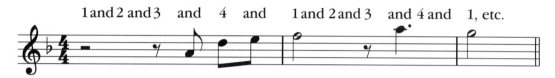

Eventually you will probably be able to dispense with counting the 'and'.
The symbol ⁊ is a **quaver rest**, worth half a beat. The note which follows it in the second bar is a **dotted crotchet**, worth one and a half beats. The off-beat dotted crotchet can therefore also be written:

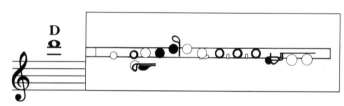

A Bossa for Betty

'Sister Caroline' features off-beat entries in a jazz-quaver context. Remember that an on-beat quaver rest is worth two thirds of a beat! The off-beat quaver is therefore later than when you are playing with an even-quaver interpretation. In order to achieve the correct interpretation listen to the CD and then try scatting what the flute is playing using the syllables written between the staves.

39

Sister Caroline

'Happy Feet' is rhythmically influenced by **Reggae**, a dance style which originated in Jamaica.

At the end of this piece you can improvise using either of the given scales, the second of which you may recognize as the blues scale starting on D.

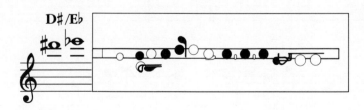

Happy Feet

Reggae ♩ = 128 (Swing ♪s)

Improvise using these scales

fade out

CHAPTER 15

The Dotted Crotchet Followed by a Quaver

The new rhythm that you will meet in this chapter is the dotted crotchet followed by a quaver. The exercises overleaf will help you to understand how this rhythm relates to previous rhythms you have learnt. They should be performed using both even- and jazz-quaver interpretations. It is particularly important that you count the beat immediately preceding the off-beat quaver.

N.B. (b) and (c), and (e) and (f) are identical rhythmically but notated differently.

Aikido

41

Red Alert

Medium Blues ♩ = 158

Fine

D.S. al Fine

Modes

The improvised solo at the end of 'I Will Call You' uses the Phrygian **mode**. A mode is another name for a scale. Using the notes of each major scale it is possible to create six additional scales or modes using each different degree of the scale as the 'home' note. Playing the E♭ major scale starting on the third degree produces G Phrygian. This mode is highly evocative of Spanish music, which has inspired such famous jazz musicians as Gil Evans, Miles Davis and Chick Corea.

I Will Call You

♩ = 124 (Swing ♪s)

D.C. al Coda

CODA

Improvise using this scale (G Phrygian):

fade out

FURTHER STUDY

Listening:

MILES DAVIS, 'Flamenco Sketches' from *Kind of Blue*, one of the first recordings to explore modal improvisation. This is perhaps the most famous example of the use of the Phrygian mode in jazz.

MILES DAVIS with the GIL EVANS ORCHESTRA, *Sketches of Spain*.

CHICK COREA, 'Spain', 'Señor Mouse' and 'Armando's Rhumba' from *Chick Corea*.

Playing/Singing:

Listen to 'So What' from MILES DAVIS' *Kind of Blue*. The rhythm of the answering phrase played by the saxophones and trumpet in response to the bass figure is a dotted crotchet followed by a quaver. Try first singing and then playing this phrase along with the recording.

CHAPTER 16

Low C and C♯

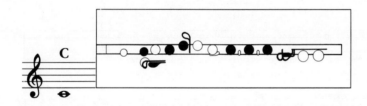 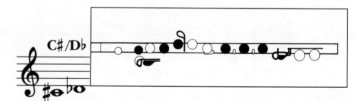

The lowest notes on the flute present a considerable technical challenge. The muscles around the diaphragm have to work harder to support the longer vibrating column of air and the fingerings for low C and C♯ demand considerable strength, dexterity and coordination from the third and fourth fingers of the right hand.

As if all this were not enough, tiny leaks higher up the instrument can easily make the very lowest tones difficult to produce without resorting to the use of excessive finger pressure, so make sure your instrument has been tested and found to be leak-free by a teacher, professional player or woodwind technician before proceeding further.

You should now incorporate long notes on C and C♯ into your daily warm-up. You may find it helpful to bear in mind the following points when attempting to produce these notes:

● Maintain firm support for the breath with the muscles around the diaphragm.

● For the lowest notes remember that you should cover less of the embouchure hole—usually no more than one quarter. You can check this using a mirror. In order to ensure that the air jet is split in half it will therefore be necessary to blow **across** more.

● These notes often tend to be excessively breathy, flat in pitch and lacking projection. You can counteract this by pushing these notes almost to the point where they break up into the octave above.

The Bottom Line

2/2 or Cut Time

The next piece is written in 2/2 time, meaning that you should count two minim beats to a bar. All notes and rests therefore have half their value in 4/4 time. For example, a crotchet is worth half a beat. Sometimes this time signature is indicated by ₵ , which stands for cut time.

Oh When the Saints Go Marching In

Traditional arranged
by John O'Neill

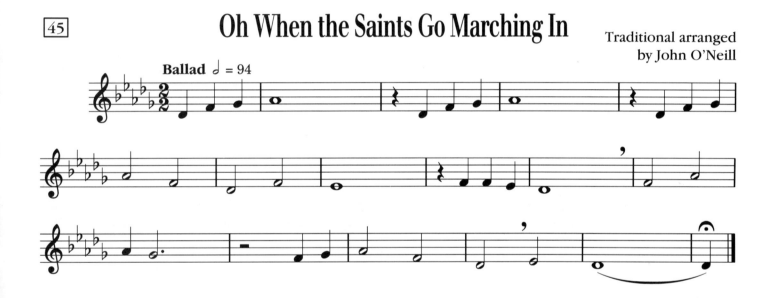

Claret and Blue

Try improvising over the backing track to 'Claret and Blue' using the blues scale (see p. 51) starting on A:

Scale Practice:

Play the scale of C major (see Chapter 11) over two octaves, starting on low C.

CHAPTER 17

Construction of Major and Minor Scales

The illustration shows the distances between the component notes of the scale of C major, measured in tones and semitones. Semitones have already been discussed (see Chapter 4, p. 26). A tone is equal to two semitones. Do not be confused by the word tone. It has three possible meanings:

1. A means of expressing a particular distance between one note and another—as in the previous paragraph.
2. Sound, with special reference to quality, e.g. 'You have been trying to achieve a good **tone** on the flute'.
3. In American usage 'tone' is synonymous with the 'note', e.g. 'Play the first three **tones** of the C major scale'.

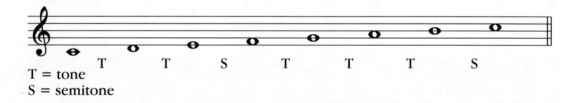

T = tone
S = semitone

Although the number of sharps or flats is different for every major scale the interrelationship of the notes is always the same. The sequence is always T T S T T T S.

For harmonic minor scales the sequence is as follows:

Notice the interval of a tone plus a semitone between the sixth and seventh degrees which gives the scale its exotic 'Middle Eastern' quality.

Interrelationship of Major and Minor Scales

The diagram opposite will help you to understand how the major and minor scales relate to one another.

It is called a cycle of fourths/fifths because the distance between each scale and the next one in the cycle is a perfect fifth if measured downwards and a perfect fourth if measured upwards.*

It is important to note the following points about the cycle:

1. The direction of movement is **clockwise**, following a fundamental tendency of chords to move by intervals of a fourth upwards or a fifth downwards.

2. It is a cycle of increasing 'flatness' or decreasing 'sharpness', proceeding from one to seven flats, and from seven to one sharps.

3. Each major scale contains only one altered note in comparison with the previous scale in the cycle. This is the fourth note of the new scale, which is flattened by one semitone. For example, the only difference between C and F major is the Bb.

4. Sharps and flats cannot be mixed in the key signature.

5. Each harmonic minor scale starts on the sixth degree of its relative major and contains the same notes except for the seventh note which is raised by one semitone. The seventh note of both major and minor scales is often referred to as the **leading note** because of its tendency to lead back to the key note.

Cycle of 4ths/5ths

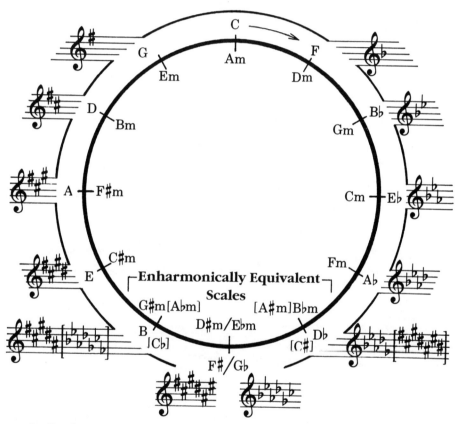

Enharmonic Scales

Notice the three enharmonic scales. Each of these scales can be thought of in two different ways (see Chapter 5, p. 28). The example below illustrates this. The scales are written differently but sound the same.

*For more information on intervals see the section on 'Ear Training', p. 39.

Practising the Scales

Start with C major and A minor scales and arpeggios and proceed through the cycle.

Practise the scales over the entire range and not simply from keynote to keynote. Flute technique is more difficult at the extremes of the instrument, so it is essential that you practise in these registers constantly, otherwise your effective range will be limited.

Start on the lowest available key-note, play up to the highest note in that scale which you are able to play, down to the lowest note in the scale on the instrument and then back up to finish where you started, The example below shows how this would apply to the G major scale and arpeggio.

Scale Variations

I would suggest practising each scale with its arpeggio and relative minor scale and arpeggio every day for at least a week. Once you have mastered the basic scale you should start to practise variations. Below are just two examples in the key of G major:

You should also experiment with many different rhythms and articulations. The possibilities are endless. The complaint that scales are boring only comes from the unimaginative! If you want to learn to improvise you must learn to be creative in your practice.

FURTHER STUDY

Playing:

In order to make your practice of major and minor scales and arpeggios more enjoyable I strongly recommend that you purchase Volume 24 of Jamey Aebersold's play-along series, entitled 'Major and Minor', which contains backing tracks for all keys. However, please be aware that Jamey uses a different form of the minor scale—the Dorian minor (see the next chapter). Appendix 2 contains further details about this series of play-alongs.

On-Beat Quaver Followed by Two Off-Beats

Another extremely common rhythm in jazz is the on-beat quaver followed by two consecutive off-beats. This may be encountered in various 'disguises' as will be apparent from the following exercises.

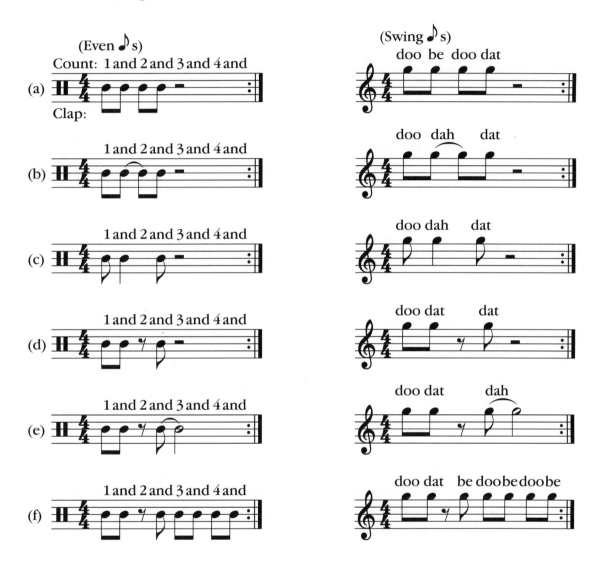

N.B. When clapped (b), (c), (d) and (e) sound the same, since the difference between them is only the *duration* of the notes and not their rhythmic position.

The instruction *8va ad lib.* at the beginning of 'Country Road' means that this piece may also be played an octave higher.

Country Road

47

'Euphrates' uses the modes of D Dorian (scale of C major starting on D) and E♭ Dorian (scale of D♭ major starting on E♭). This scale may be thought of as a variation of the minor scale since the first five notes are identical with those of the harmonic minor. It is the most commonly used mode in jazz.

Ascending Melodic Minor Scale

This composition also introduces the **ascending melodic minor** scale. This is another variation of the minor scale in which the sixth note is raised by one semitone. Another way of thinking of it is as a major scale with the third note lowered one semitone*.

*Classical musicians use a different form of the melodic minor scale in which the sixth and seventh notes are lowered by a semitone as it descends, i.e:

Jazz musicians prefer to use the notes of the ascending form whether the scale is played rising or falling, hence the name by which it is known.

It is quite possible that you may get lost in your improvisation to begin with. If this happens try the following sequence of exercises:

1. Play the CD and count carefully through each eight-bar section.
2. Play a solo in semibreves only—one note to each bar. This will give you time to count the bars.
3. Play a solo using only minims.
4. Play a solo using only crotchets.

Practising in this way will help you develop your 'internal clock' which measures the passing of time in music. Eventually you will be able to 'feel' a two-, four-, or eight-bar phrase without actually counting it.

'Endless Night' is an example of the tango, a passionate Argentinian dance-form. Like other South American dances it requires an even-quaver interpretation.

Endless Night

FURTHER STUDY

Listening:

MILES DAVIS, 'So What' from *Kind of Blue*. This is a celebrated example of the use of the Dorian mode in jazz.

CHAPTER

19

Consecutive Off-Beats

You are already familiar with rhythms which involve two consecutive off-beats (Chapter 18, p. 63), but it is not uncommon to find a whole string of them. When playing even quavers consecutive off-beats can be counted as follows:

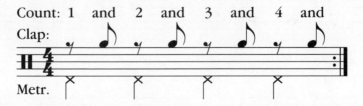

With jazz quavers counting becomes more problematic. At slow tempos you could adopt the following approach:

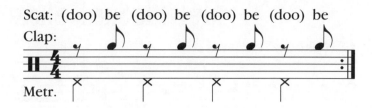

Scat: (doo) be (doo) be (doo) be (doo) be
Clap:
Metr.

However, at faster tempos there is no space to count the on-beat (see Chapter 13: Anticipation, p. 51) and you will have to rely on developing the correct 'feel'.

Perform the previous exercise setting the metronome at about 80 beats per minute and gradually increasing the tempo to 160.

You will probably notice one of two tendencies as the tempo increases: either the off-beat quaver becomes even rather than swung, which is a sign of rushing or playing ahead of the beat, or the off-beat gets closer and closer to the following beat, which is symptomatic of playing late or behind the beat. You will also notice a point where to say the 'doo' begins to feel uncomfortable and rushed; so dispense with vocalizing the on-beat and try to feel the rhythm.

'My Little Suede Shoes' (overleaf) is one of Charlie Parker's most famous compositions and one of the earliest examples of the calypso rhythm in jazz. The calypso is a dance form which originated in Trinidad. It is characterized by a strong 'two-in-the-bar' feeling, which is achieved by the bass playing mainly on the first and third beats of each bar.

Charlie Parker

My Little Suede Shoes

50

Charlie Parker

Calypso ♩ = 158 (Even ♪s)

D.S. al Coda

'Doxy' was written by Sonny Rollins (b. 1929), who established himself in the band led by drummer Max Roach and trumpeter Clifford Brown and whose unmistakable tone, and unique sense of phrasing and rhythm make him one of the greatest jazz soloists.

Doxy

51

Sonny Rollins

Medium ♩ = 120 (Swing ♪s)

Andy Panayi (b. 1964) studied flute and composition at Trinity College of Music, London and is also an accomplished saxophonist. He is active on the jazz scene as a leader of his own groups and as a member of other ensembles including the Dankworth Generation Band. He won the Marty Paich arranging prize in the BBC Big Band Competition of 1987. He can be heard on the accompanying CD.

I'm In Love

Andrew Panayi

CODA
Improvise using this scale (B♭ mixolydian)

FURTHER STUDY

Listening:

CHARLIE PARKER, 'My Little Suede Shoes' from *Charlie Parker*.
SONNY ROLLINS, 'Doxy' from *Prestige Years Vol. 2*.

CHAPTER 20

Triplet Crotchets

Triplet crotchets are exactly twice the length of triplet quavers and therefore involve grouping three notes against two beats. The following clapping exercise will help you to understand the relationship between triplet quavers and triplet crotchets:

Once you have mastered the above try this exercise for tapping triplet crotchets against regular crotchets:

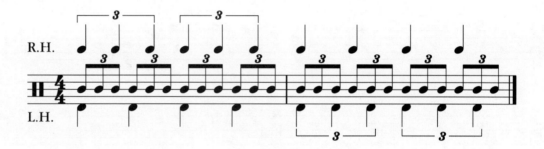

The triplet quavers have been written to enable you to work out the rhythm mathematically but you should aim at being able to count the crotchet pulse and 'feel' the triplet crotchet rhythm.

Triplet crotchets should be played absolutely evenly—a common fault is to play the second one early and the third one late so that the rhythm resembles ♪♩ ♪ rather than ♩♩♩.

The final section of 'Tango Cool' will give you a good opportunity to differentiate these two rhythms.

Tango Cool

Ted Gioia

Eric Dolphy

Frankincense

Don Rendell

'Peace' was written by Horace Silver (b. 1928), who first received public acclaim as a member of Miles Davis' rhythm section of the early 1950s and later became famous as a composer and bandleader in his own right.

55   # Peace

Horace Silver

Horace Silver

So far you have improvised using different scales. The next piece gives you the opportunity to improvise with a sequence of three arpeggios—C, F and G major, indicated by the symbols C, F and G. Play just the arpeggio notes to begin with. In other words in the first bar you can play either C, E or G, in the second bar F, A or C and in the third bar, G, B or D. This sounds simple enough but you will discover that it is quite a challenge to keep track of where you are in the sequence. If you find that you keep losing your place try playing just the lowest note of each arpeggio until you begin to feel the rhythm in which the chords are moving.

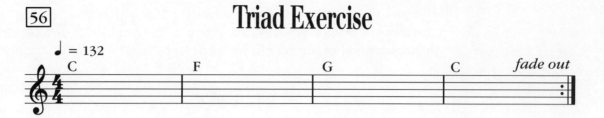

Triad Exercise

♩ = 132

C   F   G   C   *fade out*

FURTHER STUDY

Listening:

TED GIOIA/MARK LEWIS, 'Tango Cool' from *Tango Cool.*
HORACE SILVER, 'Peace' from *Blowin' the Blues Away.*

CHAPTER   21

Since the early 1960s there has been increasing experimentation with time signatures other than 3/4 or 4/4 in jazz. Pianist Dave Brubeck, alto saxophonist Paul Desmond and trumpeter Don Ellis were among the first to experiment widely with unusual time signatures.

Dave Brubeck Quartet

6/8 Time

6/8 time means that you count six quavers to a bar, although at faster tempos this is nearly always counted in two (dotted-crotchet beats), with each beat subdivided into three. The exercises below show both possibilities for counting.

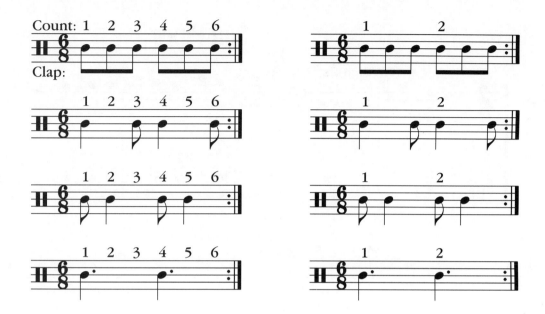

'Mingus-Thingus' is written in the bluesy 6/8 style often favoured by the great double bass player and composer Charles Mingus (1922–1979).

The instruction **Rit.** is short for 'ritardando', an Italian word meaning 'holding back'. It therefore means the same as 'rallentando', which you encountered in Chapter 11.

5/4 Time

Like many of the more complex time signatures, such as 7/4 or 11/4, 5/4 is nearly always subdivided into a combination of two- and three-beat groupings. You will probably find it easier to count these groups of two or three rather than the actual number of beats in the bar. In 'Pan Pipes' the subdivision is three followed by two.

The instruction **tacet** means literally 'is silent'. In other words the lower part only joins in at the end of the first time bar.

In the improvised section at the end you could also use the F blues scale (F, A♭, B♭, C♭ (=B), C and E♭).

58 # Pan Pipes

Irregular Phrasing

Irregular phrasing occurs when a phrase is repeated in unpredictable positions within the bar. In 'Straight, No Chaser' the phrasing is completely asymmetrical, making it very difficult to know where the 'one' is. Careful counting is the only solution.

Straight, No Chaser

Thelonious Monk

FURTHER STUDY

Listening:

CHARLES MINGUS, 'Better Git It In Your Soul' from *Mingus Ah Um*. A fine example of the use of 6/8 time in jazz.

DAVE BRUBECK, *Time Out*. Features Paul Desmond's composition 'Take Five', one of the most famous tunes in an unusual time signature.

THELONIOUS MONK, 'Straight, No Chaser' from *The Composer*.

Playing:

LOESBERG, JOHN, ed., *An Irish Tunebook* Parts One and Two. These books contain much enjoyable and exciting music in 6/8 time. They also provide excellent practice for technique, rhythm and articulation and good source material for playing by ear and transposition.

Harmony

Up until now your attempts at improvisation have largely been confined to different scales or modes. In order to become a complete musician you will also have to study **harmony**. Harmony is concerned with *simultaneous* sounds. It is one of the three great building blocks of music—the others being **rhythm**, or the organization of notes in time, and **melody**, which deals with the ordering of *successive* sounds. It is not the intention of this book to deal with harmony in depth but rather to whet your appetite.

In Chapter 8 you were introduced to the idea of a triad. You can form a triad by taking any note of any major or minor scale and adding diatonic notes at intervals of a third. (Diatonic notes are those which belong to the scale in question.) Observe that the notes will either all be written on lines or all on spaces:

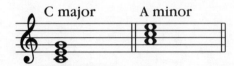

This procedure of building chords by stacking up notes in thirds can be extended to as many as seven notes, in which case all the notes in the scale are being played simultaneously. The example below shows a rearrangement of the notes of the C major scale.

If you have access to a piano and rudimentary knowledge of the keyboard you will benefit by exploring some of these exotic possibilities. If not, you should consider taking up the keyboard as a second study. Many jazz musicians have found that knowledge of the keyboard opens up exciting new possibilities in improvisation. Dizzy Gillespie, Bob Brookmeyer and Gerry Mulligan are just three famous examples.

Diatonic Chords

In modern jazz the four-note chord (with added seventh) is the basic unit of harmony. It is therefore important for you to get to know the diatonic four-note chords in each major and harmonic minor scale. Below are examples for the keys of C major and A minor.

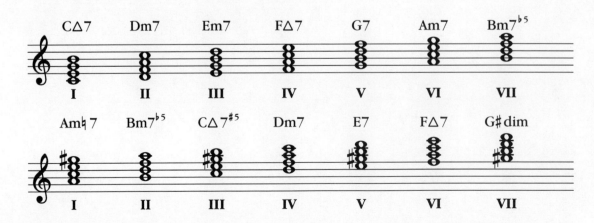

Chord Symbols

Below each chord is a Roman numeral which identifies the scale degree on which it is based. Written above each chord is a **chord symbol**, which is a kind of harmonic shorthand used by jazz musicians to identify different chord types. You need not know all of these at present. The following are the most important:

△7   =   major seventh (major triad + major seventh measured from lowest note)
7   =   seventh (major triad + minor seventh)
m7   =   minor seventh (minor triad + minor seventh)
m7$^{\flat5}$ =   minor seventh with a flattened fifth. This chord is indicated by some jazz educators with the symbol Ø

The following tune will serve as a model in this exploration of jazz harmony.

Fall '90

Below if the chord progression to 'Fall '90'

If you look at the direction of movement or **resolution** of the chords you will see that much of the time it follows the direction of the cycle of fourths/fifths (p. 61).

II-V-I Progression

The harmony of this tune largely consists of movement from the II chord to the V chord to the I chord in the keys of C major and A minor.* This is the **II-V-I progression**, by far the most common chord progression in jazz.

The following sequence of exercises will help to familiarize you with the chord progression of 'Fall '90'. It may take you a long time to master them, but please persevere—the knowledge you gain will sharpen your ear and help your improvisation to become more sophisticated. A similar sequence of exercises could be used for learning the harmony of any standard tune.

N.B. Chords are written for reference only. All these exercises should be memorized and played by ear.

● Sing and then play the **root** progression. The root is the scale degree on which the chord is built. There are different ways of performing this exercise, since you have a choice of whether you move up or down to the next note, e.g.:

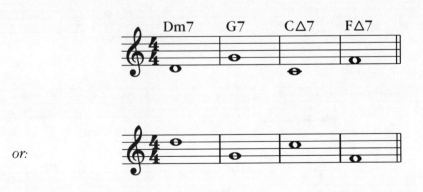

or:

* The Am6 chord (A-C-E-F♯) has been substituted for the Am♭7 but its harmonic function is the same.

● Sing and play the chord progression, one note to each beat, e.g.:

N.B. For the bars with two chords you should play just the root and the third, e.g.:

The arpeggios can also be played descending, e.g.:

As a further variation, the arpeggio shapes could be transposed to different registers of the instrument. This principle could also be applied to the exercises which follow.

Voice-Leading

● Improvise a melodic line in semibreves, using chord notes only. This is an excellent exercise for **voice-leading**, or the smooth connection of one chord with another. It is usually better to move from one chord to the next by moving in small steps, although bigger intervals can be used for dramatic effect. Feel free to repeat notes if they are common to both chords, e.g.:

● Improvise a line in minims, using chord notes only, e.g.:

● Improvise in crotchets using chord notes only. This is closely related to the 'walking bass' technique used by jazz bass-players. You may need to make room for breathing spaces, by leaving out notes here and there, e.g.:

● Improvise in free rhythm using chord notes only, e.g.:

● Improvise freely using additional notes from the C major and A minor scales and any others which sound good!

FURTHER STUDY

Playing:

JERRY COKER, *Jerry Coker's Jazz Keyboard*. An excellent book for developing jazz keyboard skills, for pianists and non-pianists.

LIONEL GRIGSON, *Practical Jazz*. A thorough exploration of jazz harmony and its relevance for improvisation.

CHAPTER 23

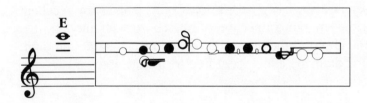

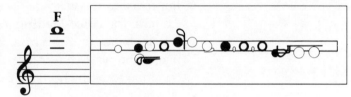

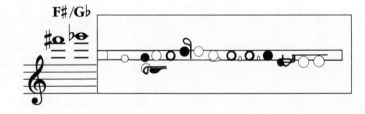

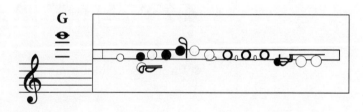

This chapter introduces E, F, F♯ and G from the high register of the flute. It can be taxing both for the lips and the fingers to play in this area of the instrument, E and F♯ being particularly difficult to produce. Some instruments have a so-called 'split E' mechanism, which facilitates the blowing of this note. However, it unfortunately also tends to make the F♯ harder to achieve, so should not necessarily be regarded as the solution to the problem! When playing these higher notes it will be helpful to bear in mind the following points:

● Maintain support for the air column at all times.

● Keep the throat open and relaxed.

● The aperture between the lips should be as small as possible.

● You need to cover approximately two thirds of the embouchure hole with your lower lip.

● In order to continue to split the air-jet in half it will be necessary to blow more downwards.

Harmonics/Overtones

One of the most effective ways of developing an awareness of the changes in the embouchure which are necessary over the range of the flute is to practise blowing **harmonics**, or **overtones**, which are secondary tones sounding within a basic note, known as the **fundamental**. It is the difference in the combination of overtones, or harmonic spectrum, which explains the difference in timbre between different musical instruments. In fact, without realizing it, you have already been playing overtones, since all the notes above middle D are harmonics of notes below!

In the following exercises you should finger the lowest or fundamental note all the time and attempt to produce the upper notes or overtones by varying the angle and speed of the air-jet and the distance between the lips and the far edge of the embouchure hole. It is essential that you really imagine the sound of the overtones in your head. If you find it difficult to do this first play the note using the 'official' fingering and then try producing it using the harmonic fingering. These are excellent warm-up exercises.

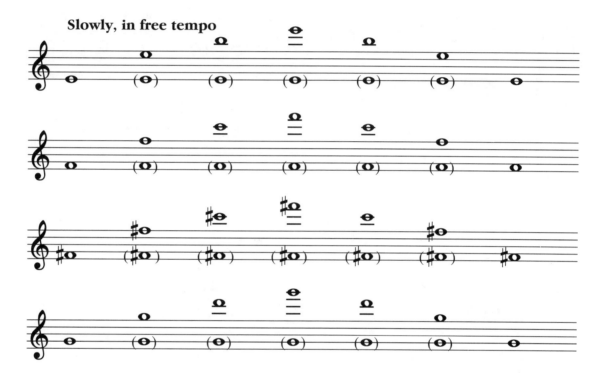

You should also incorporate one or two of the following finger exercises into your daily warm-up:

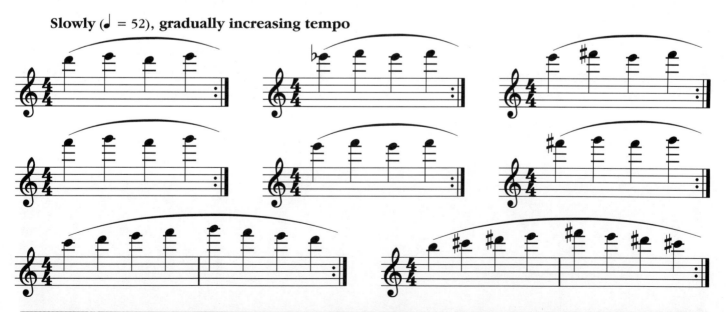

'Danny Boy', also known as the 'Londonderry Air' is a traditional Irish tune which has attracted many jazz musicians, including Ben Webster and Bill Evans.

61

Danny Boy

Traditional arranged by
John O'Neill and Phil Lee

Although the next two pieces are both in cut time (see Chapter 16 p. 59) it may help you to work out the rhythms if you begin by counting four to a bar.

62

St Thomas

Sonny Rollins

'Blue Samba' is a composition by Lee Konitz (b. 1926), who started his professional career in the band of Claude Thornhill and, after studying with Lennie Tristano, developed into one of the most creative improvisors in jazz. Lee requested this tune to be written in fifteen keys (including the three enharmonic keys). That would be an interesting project for you!

'Blue Samba' is an example of the samba rhythm which, like the bossa nova, is a dance style originating from Brazil. It is the samba sound which is at the heart of the famous carnival which takes place every year in the streets of Rio de Janeiro.

Blue Samba

Lee Konitz

FURTHER STUDY

Playing:

Take any of the tunes you have played so far and transpose them to the high register of the instrument. Apparently 'simple' tunes can become very awkward when moved to a different register of the instrument!

Listening:

BEN WEBSTER, 'Danny Boy' from *King of the Tenors*.
SONNY ROLLINS, 'St. Thomas' from *Tenor Madness/Saxophone Colossus*.
LEE KONITZ, 'Blue Samba' from *Zounds*.

CHAPTER 24

Semiquavers and Semiquaver Rests

Semiquavers, or sixteenth notes, are half the length of even quavers. Rhythms which involve semiquavers can look very complicated—suddenly the manuscript becomes very black!—but try not to be intimidated. If you look carefully at the rhythm exercises below you will see that the mathematical relationship between the notes in the semiquaver examples in 2/4 is the same as in the quaver examples in 4/4 which are written next to them. It is only the unit of time that you are counting which changes.

For this reason you may initially find it helpful to count the quaver beat when playing semiquaver rhythms. This means that the first example would be counted as follows:

Another option would be to count like this:

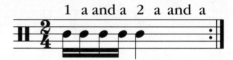

You could apply the same principle to the other exercises, but work towards being able to count crotchet beats.

The sign ⁊ is a semiquaver rest.

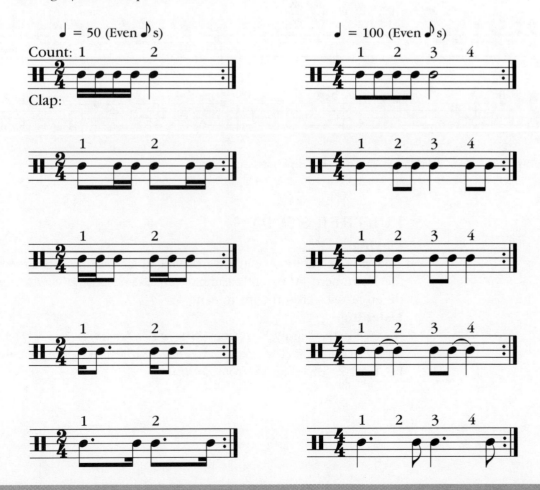

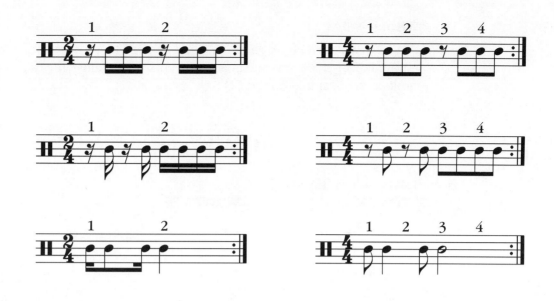

Drumming exercise

The following exercise will provide excellent practice both for rhythm and articulation. It should be played for a few minutes at each practice session as part of your warm-up until you have mastered it. Play it on various notes throughout the range.

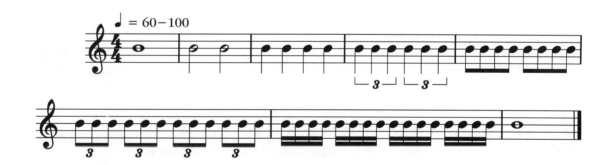

Grace Notes

The G♯ written before the A in bars 12 and 15 of 'It's All Yours' is a **grace note**. It should be played on the beat and 'crushed' against the note which follows. Try to imitate the example on the CD.

64

It's All Yours

In the improvised section of the following piece you could also use the G blues scale (G, B♭, C, D♭, D and F).

On the Street

65

Improvise using these scales until fade:

C Mixolydian   G Dorian

Part Three: Appendices

BIBLIOGRAPHY

The following publications are those to which specific reference is made in the sections entitled Further Study.

BERENDT, JOACHIM E. *The Jazz Book* (London, Paladin, 1984). Useful both as a reference book and as an introduction to the subject.

COKER, JERRY. *Jerry Coker's Jazz Keyboard* (Florida, Columbia Pictures Publications, 1984)

GIDDINS, GARY. *Celebrating Bird: The Triumph of Charlie Parker* (New York, Beech Tree Books, William Morrow and Company, Inc., 1987)

GRIGSON, LIONEL. *Practical Jazz* (London, Stainer and Bell, 1988)

HINDEMITH, PAUL. *Elementary Training for Musicians* (Mainz, Schott, 1946)

KERNFELD, BARRY, ed. *The New Grove Dictionary of Jazz* (Macmillan Press, 1988). A significant investment but worth every penny. The most complete and authoritative reference work on the subject.

REISNER, ROBERT. *Bird: The Legend of Charlie Parker* (New York, Citadel Press, 1962)

RUSSELL, ROSS. *Bird Lives* (New York, Charterhouse, 1973)

SADIE, STANLEY, ed. *The New Grove Dictionary of Music and Musicians* (London, Macmillan, 1980)

STOKES, SHERIDAN, W. and CONDON, RICHARD A. *Illustrated Method for Flute* (Culver City, California, Trio Associates)

These books are recommended for general background and interest:

ARDLEY, NEIL. *Music: An Illustrated Encyclopedia* (London, Hamlyn Publishing, 1986). A useful general reference work.

GIOIA, TED. *The Imperfect Art* (New York, Oxford University Press, 1988). A unique and thought-provoking discussion on the place of jazz in modern culture.

GRIME, KITTY. *Jazz at Ronnie Scott's* (London, Robert Hale, 1979). A fascinating collection of anecdotes and aphorisms by musicians who have played at the club.

HENTOFF, NAT and SHAPIRO, NAT. *Hear Me Talkin' to Ya: the Story of Jazz by the Men Who Made It* (New York, Rinehart, 1955). Complements perfectly the Kitty Grime book mentioned above.

The books below are recommended as supplementary or additional material:

BACH, J.S. trans. GUENTHER, RALPH. *The Flutist's Bach* (Miami, Belwin Inc.). Transcribed from the works for solo violin and cello, these studies are masterpieces of melodic invention. Intermediate to advanced.

GERSHWIN, GEORGE, arr. DE SMET. *The Music of George Gershwin for flute* (London, Wise Publications, 1987). Beautiful melodies, of beginner to intermediate standard, suitable for reading or learning by heart.

GIUFFRE, JIMMY. *Jazz Phrasing and Interpretation* (New York, Associated Music Publishers, 1969). A thorough exploration of this subject by a woodwind player who is one of the great voices of jazz and a highly respected teacher.

KERN, JEROME, arr. DE SMET. *The Music of Jerome Kern for Flute* (London, Wise Publications). Of similar value to the Gershwin book noted above.

LATEEF, YUSEF. *Flute Book of the Blues* (Teaneck, New Jersey, The Alnur Music Company, 1965). Effectively a set of thirty six variations on The Blues in various keys, this book presents an enjoyable way to develop 'feel' and sight-reading skills in the jazz idiom.

RAE, JAMES. *Progressive Jazz Studies for Flute – Easy Level* (London, Faber Music). Useful supplementary material for developing reading skills.

RENDELL, DON. *Robbins Flute Tutor Part Two* (London, Robbins Music Corporation Limited, 1972). This book contains many studies and exercises for developing tone and technique, particularly in the high register, and improvisational skill, and is recommended for students moving on from this book.

SHANAPHY, ED, and ISACOFF, STUART. *Dick Hyman's Professional Chord Changes and Substitutions For 100 Tunes Every Musician Should Know* (New York, Ekay Music, 1986). Valuable for building a repertoire of tunes. The melodies and chords are accurate and there is the added bonus of lyrics, which are indispensable for learning how to phrase a tune properly.

WONG, HERB, ed. *The Ultimate Jazz Fake Book* (Winona, Hal Leonard Publishing Corporation, 1988). Like the Dick Hyman book, this is an excellent source of tunes to learn and also contains lyrics.

APPENDIX 2

DISCOGRAPHY

Every effort has been made to ensure that this discography is as up to date and accurate as possible at the time of writing, but since recordings are being deleted and reissued all the time it is impossible to guarantee that all are currently available. Similarly, if a recording is not listed in the format you require, e.g. CD, record or cassette, you should not jump to the conclusion that it is permanently unavailable in that format.

Should you find it difficult to obtain any of the recordings, try looking in one of the many specialist jazz record shops, most of which have second-hand sections and also import recordings from other countries.

This discography was compiled with the expert assistance of Bob Glass of Ray's Jazz Shop Ltd, 180 Shaftesbury Avenue, London.

Key: CD = compact disc; LP = long-playing record; C = cassette

ARMSTRONG, LOUIS. *Hot 5 and Hot 7 (1925–1928)* (Giants of Jazz GOJCD 0242 [CD])

BAKER, CHET. *The Touch of Your Lips* (Steeplechase SCS-1122 [LP])

BASIE, COUNT. *Swinging the Blues* (That's Jazz TJCD 0004 [CD], TJMC 0004 [C, LP])

BRUBECK, DAVE. *Time Out* (CBS [Sony Music] 4606111 [LP], 4606112 [CD], 4604114 [C])

CHRISTIAN, CHARLIE. *The Genius of the Electric Guitar* from the CBS Jazz Masterpieces series (CBS [Sony Music] 4606122 [CD], 4606121 [LP], 4606124 [C])

CLIFF, DAVE. *The Right Time* (Miles Music MM074 [LP])

COLETTE, BUDDY quintet featuring JAMES NEWTON. *Flute Talk* (Soul Note 121 165-2 [CD])

COREA, CHICK. *Return to Forever* (ECM 1022 811978-2 [CD])

—*Light as a Feather* (Polydor 827 148-2 [CD])

Both the above recordings feature the flute playing of Joe Farrell.

DAVIS, MILES. *Kind of Blue* (CBS [Sony Music] CD 62066 [CD], 62066 [LP])

—*Sketches of Spain* (CBS [Sony Music] CD 62327 [CD], 40320223 [C, LP])

EVANS, BILL. *At the Village Vanguard* (London Records FCD 60017 [CD])

FITZGERALD, ELLA. *Sings the Duke Ellington Songbook* (Verve [Polygram] 8370352 [CD])

GETZ, STAN. *Jazz Samba* (Verve [Polydor] 8100611 [LP], 8100612 [CD], 8100614 [C])

—*Stan Getz and Joao Gilberto* (Verve [Polydor] 810048 2 [CD] 230 407 1 [LP])

GIOIA, TED. *The End of the Open Road* (Quartet Q-1001-CD [CD])
—with LEWIS, MARK. *Tango Cool* (Quartet QCD 1006 [CD])
HORN, PAUL. *The Jazz Years* (Black Sun 15015-2 [CD])
JARREAU, AL. *Breakin' Away* (Warner Bros 256917 [CD])
KIRK ROLAND. *Petite Fleur* (Moon Records MCD 027-2 [CD])
KONITZ, LEE. *Zounds* (Soul Note SN 121-219-2 [CD])
LATEEF, YUSEF. *Eastern Sounds* (Prestige OJCCD-612-2 (P-7319) [CD])
LAWS, HUBERT. *My Time Will Come* (Music Masters 01612-65100-2 [CD])
MANN, HERBIE. *Memphis Underground* (Atlantic 7567 81364-2 [CD])
MANN, HERBIE and JASPAR, BOBBY. *Flute Soufflé* (Prestige OJCCD-760-2 (P-7101) [CD])
McFERRIN, BOBBY. *Spontaneous Inventions* (Blue Note CDP 7462982 [CD], BN2 57 [C], BT 85110 [LP])
MINGUS, CHARLES. *Mingus Ah-Um* (CBS [Sony Music] 4504361 [LP], 4504362 [CD], 4504364 [C])
MOODY, JAMES. *Moving Forward* (Novus PD 83026 [CD])
MONK, THELONIOUS. *The Composer* from the Contemporary Jazz Masterpieces series (CBS [Sony Music] 463382 or CK 44297 [CD], 4633384 or CJT 44927 [C/LP])
NEW YORK JAZZ QUARTET. *The New York Jazz Quartet* (Sonet SNTCD 753 [CD]). Features Frank Wess on flute.
PARKER, CHARLIE. *Charlie Parker* in the Compact Jazz and Walkman Jazz series (Verve [Polygram] 8332882 [CD] 8332884 [C])
—*Bird Symbols* (Rhapsody [President] RHCD 5 [CD], RHAP 5 [LP])
—*The Best of Bird on Savoy* (Vogue VG655 650109 [CD])
ROLLINS, SONNY. *Prestige Years Vol. 2 (1954–1956)* (Prestige PRE 4002 [CD])
—*Tenor Madness/Saxophone Colossus* (Prestige [Ace] CDJZD 002 [CD])
SHANK, BUD and ALMEIDA, LAURINDO. *Baa-Too-Kee* (Giants of Jazz CD 53133 [CD])
SILVER, HORACE. *Blowin' the Blues Away* (Blue Note/EMI BN2 89/CDP 7465212 [CD], 4BN 84017 [C], BST 84017 [LP])
STEIG, JEREMY and GOMEZ, EDDIE. *Outlaws* (Enja 2098 [LP])
TABACKIN, LEW. *Desert Lady* (Concord CCD 4411 [CD])
VARIOUS. *All Night Long* (Prestige LP 7073 [LP]). Features Jerome Richardson on flute.
WEBSTER, BEN. *King of the Tenors* (Verve 837 437-1 [CD])

Charles Lloyd

Mention should also be made of the series of play-a-long CDs, records and cassettes produced by the American jazz educator **Jamey Aebersold**. There are, at the time of writing, 56 of these featuring compositions by great jazz musicians and also many excellent 'standard' tunes. The records come complete with a booklet which includes melody, chord-progressions and sometimes lyrics. The booklets also sometimes include helpful advice on improvisation. The recordings feature a rhythm section of bass, drums and piano which provides a backing track over which you can play the tune and then improvise. These rhythm sections are made up of professional jazz musicians, often among the finest players in the world. Vol. 2 *Nothin' But The Blues* and Vol. 5 *Time To Play Music* and Vol. 54 *Maiden Voyage* are particularly suitable for students moving on from this book.

USEFUL ACCESSORIES

Cleaning Rod

In order to clean the inside of the flute and dry out the pads a small piece of soft cloth or chamois leather is inserted in the 'eye' of the cleaning rod, which is then passed through the instrument.

Watchmakers' Screwdrivers

These are useful for tightening any loose screws or making minor adjustments.

Tuning Fork

It is best to obtain an A = 440 tuning fork. The note A on your flute should be in tune with this.

Metronome

Make sure the metronome clicks loudly enough to be heard. This tends to be more of a problem with electronic metronomes than with mechanical ones.

Soft cloth

For keeping the outside of the instrument clean.

Cotton Buds

For cleaning in those places where a soft cloth cannot reach, e.g. under the rods and around the pillars.

FINGERING CHART

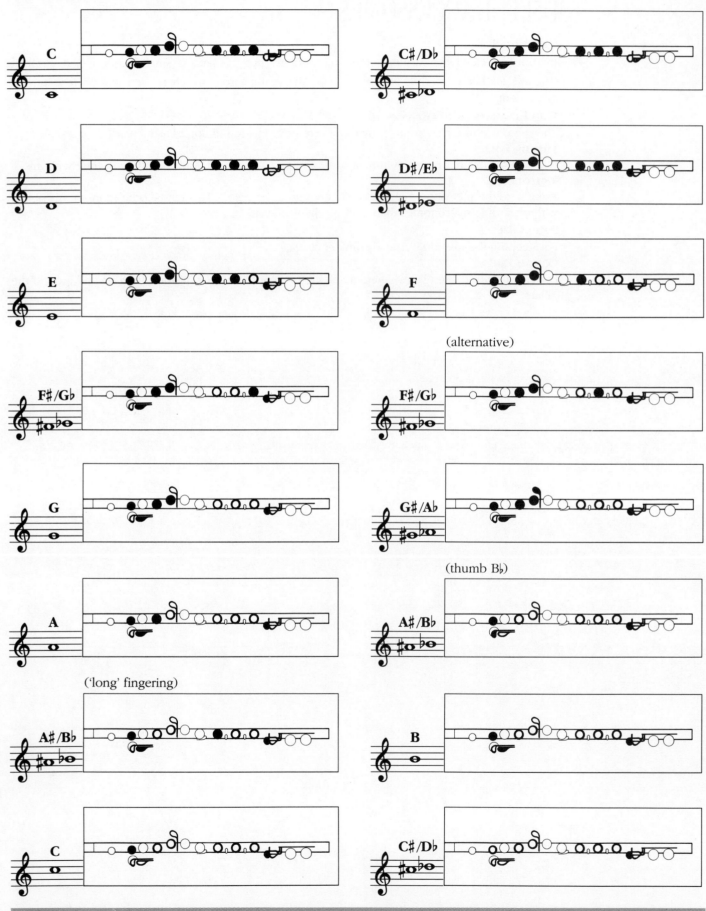

(alternative)

('long' fingering)

(thumb B♭)

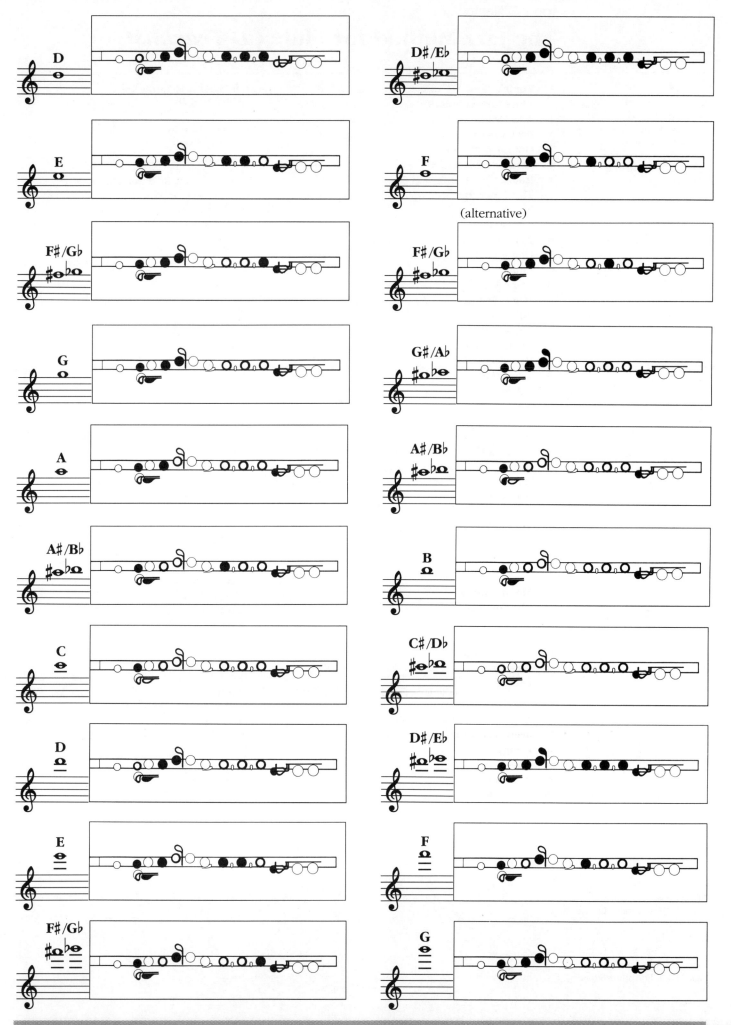

(alternative)

John O'Neill

The Jazz Method for Flute *CD Tracklist*

The Band:
Andy Panayi (Flute)
Phil Lee (Guitar)
Jeff Clyne (Double Bass)
Paul Clarvis (Drums)
All compositions by John O'Neill unless otherwise indicated

1	**Tuning Note(A)**	24
2	**Blues for Beginners**	37
3	**A La Mode**	19
4	**Progression**	34
5	**Out for the Count**	46
6	**Times Remembered**	34
7	**P.M.**	40
8	**Third Attempt**	40
9	**Flat 5**	26
10	**Interstellar**	21
11	**251**	31
12	**Home Bass**	39
13	**James**	23
14	**South View**	52
15	**Minor Problem**	38
16	**Roberto**	37
17	**Delta City**	1'00
18	**Gangsterland**	1'16
19	**Breaking Point**	22
20	**Transition**	32
21	**Sylvie's Dance**	37
22	**K.O.**	36
23	**Blue Jean**	47
24	**Improvisation in F**	1'07
25	**Devil Music**	32
26	**Bird Waltz** (C major)	39
27	**Bird Waltz** (B major)	39
28	**A Song for Sophie**	2'05
29	**The House in the Forest**	2'07
30	**Tongue-Twister**	28
31	**Lullaby** TED GIOIA © 1991, Ted Gioia. All rights reserved. Used by permission	1'36
32	**Moon Tune**	1'14
33	**The Loneliest Monk**	44
34	**Improvisation in G**	1'02
35	**The Magician**	1'08
36	**'Trane Refrain**	44
37	**Blue Monk** THELONIOUS MONK © 1962, Bocu Music Ltd. All rights reserved. Used by permission	1'35
38	**A Bossa for Betty**	1'25
39	**Sister Caroline**	45
40	**Happy Feet**	2'06
41	**Aikido**	1'17
42	**Red Alert**	1'05
43	**I Will Call You**	2'03
44	**The Bottom Line**	38
45	**Oh When the Saints Go Marching In** Trad. arr. JOHN O'NEILL	50
46	**Claret and Blue**	58
47	**Country Road**	1'13
48	**Euphrates** DON RENDELL © 1991, Don Rendell. All rights reserved. Used by permission	3'03
49	**Endless Night**	1'11
50	**My Little Suede Shoes** CHARLIE PARKER © 1956/1967, Atlantic Music Corp. Sub-published in the UK & Eire by Marada Music Ltd. All rights reserved. Used by permission	1'12
51	**Doxy** SONNY ROLLINS © 1963, Prestige Music Ltd. All rights reserved. Used by permission	37
52	**I'm in Love** ANDREW PANAYI © 1994, Andrew Panayi. All rights reserved. Used by permission	2'02
53	**Tango Cool** TED GIOIA © 1991, Ted Gioia. All rights reserved. Used by permission	1'48
54	**Frankincense** DON RENDELL © 1993, Don Rendell. All rights reserved. Used by permission	1'21
55	**Peace** HORACE SILVER © 1971 Ecaroh Music for the World. Administered by BMG Music Publishing Limited in the United Kingdom and Eire.	1'39
56	**Triad Exercise**	1'14
57	**Mingus-Thingus**	1'00
58	**Pan Pipes**	2'20
59	**Straight, No Chaser** THELONIOUS MONK © 1962, Bocu Music Ltd. All rights reserved. Used by permission	48
60	**fall '90**	1'26
61	**Danny Boy** Trad. arr. JOHN O'NEILL/PHIL LEE	1'20
62	**St Thomas** SONNY ROLLINS © 1963, Prestige Music Ltd. All rights reserved. Used by permission	48
63	**Blue Samba** LEE KONITZ © 1991, Lee Konitz. All rights reserved. Used by permission	51
64	**It's All Yours**	2'27
65	**On the Street**	3'02

Schott Educational Publications
℗ & © 1994 Schott & Co. Ltd, London
Produced by John O'Neill, Nick Taylor & Wendy Lampa
Sound Engineer:
Nick Taylor, Porcupine Studio